Frank-Jürgen Richter

Strategic Networks
The Art of Japanese Interfirm Cooperation

*Pre-publication
REVIEWS,
COMMENTARIES,
EVALUATIONS . . .*

"**T**his book is exciting to read, coming as it does in the wake of the collapse of the Japanese bubble economy and the Asian monetary crisis. What looked to be invincible massive corporations now seem to be mere edifices once supported by nepotism and unsecured bank loans. Richter draws on his broad experience to take the reader easily through a mass of detail with well-argued text—some arranged in a tidy academic fashion being well referenced, and some clearly derived from personal knowledge. All in all it builds up to an impressive document, which, far from boring the reader, continues to offer insights into the operations of the Japanese firm."

John B. Kidd
*Operations & Information Group,
Aston Business School,
Birmingham, United Kingdom*

International Business Press
An Imprint of The Haworth Press, Inc.

Strategic Networks
*The Art of Japanese
Interfirm Cooperation*

INTERNATIONAL BUSINESS PRESS
Erdener Kaynak, PhD
Executive Editor

New, Recent, and Forthcoming Titles:

How to Manage for International Competitiveness edited by Abbas J. Ali

International Business Expansion into Less-Developed Countries: The International Finance Corporation and Its Operations by James C. Baker

Product-Country Images: Impact and Role in International Marketing edited by Nicolas Papadopoulos and Louise A. Heslop

The Global Business: Four Key Marketing Strategies edited by Erdener Kaynak

Multinational Strategic Alliances edited by Refik Culpan

Market Evolution in Developing Countries: The Unfolding of the Indian Market by Subhash C. Jain

A Guide to Successful Business Relations with the Chinese: Opening the Great Wall's Gate by Huang Quanyu, Richard Andrulis, and Chen Tong

Industrial Products: A Guide to the International Marketing Economics Model by Hans Jansson

Euromarketing: Effective Strategies for International Trade and Export edited by Salah S. Hassan and Erdener Kaynak

How to Utilize New Information Technology in the Global Marketplace: A Basic Guide edited by Fahri Karakaya and Erdener Kaynak

International Negotiating: A Primer for American Business Professionals by Michael Kublin

The Eight Core Values of the Japanese Businessman: Toward an Understanding of Japanese Management by Yasutaka Sai

Implementation of Total Quality Management: A Comprehensive Training Program by Rolf E. Rogers

An International Accounting Practice Set: The Karissa Jean's Simulation by David R. Peterson and Nancy Schendel

Privatization and Entrepreneurship: The Managerial Challenge in Central and Eastern Europe by Arieh Ullmann and Alfred Lewis

U.S. Trade, Foreign Direct Investments, and Global Competitiveness by Rolf Hackmann

Business Decision Making in China by Huang Quanyu, Joseph Leonard, and Chen Tong

International Management Leadership: The Primary Competitive Advantage by Raimo W. Nurmi and John R. Darling

The Trans-Oceanic Marketing Channel: A New Tool for Understanding Tropical Africa's Export Agriculture by H. Laurens van der Laan

Handbook of Cross-Cultural Marketing by Paul A. Herbig

Guide to Software Export: A Handbook for International Software Sales by Roger Philips

Executive Development and Organizational Learning for Global Business edited by J. Bernard Keys and Robert M. Fulmer

Contextual Management: A Global Perspective by Raghbir (Raj) S. Basi

Japan and China: The Meeting of Asia's Economic Giants by Kazua John Fukuda

Export Savvy: From Basics to Strategy by Zak Karamally

Strategic Networks: The Art of Japanese Interfirm Cooperation by Frank-Jürgen Richter

Export-Import Theory, Practices, and Procedures by Belay Seyoum

Strategic Networks
The Art of Japanese Interfirm Cooperation

Frank-Jürgen Richter

International Business Press
An Imprint of The Haworth Press, Inc.
New York • London • Oxford

Published by

International Business Press®, an imprint of The Haworth Press, Inc., 10 Alice Street, Binghamton, NY 13904-1580

Cover design by Marylouise E. Doyle.

Library of Congress Cataloging-in-Publication Data

Richter, Frank-Jürgen.
    Strategic networks : the art of Japanese interfirm cooperation / Frank-Jürgen Richter.
        p.   cm.
    Includes bibliographical references and index.
    ISBN 0-7890-0725-8 (alk. paper)
    1. Corporations—Japan. 2. Interorganizational relations—Japan. I. Title.
HD2907.R53 1999
338.8′0952—dc21   99-14372
                                                                                                                    CIP

To Nadja,
who knows the spiritual foundation of networks

ABOUT THE AUTHOR

Dr. Frank-Jürgen Richter holds a senior management position with a European multinational company and works in Beijing, China. Dr. Richter has broad, high-level international management experience in Germany, Japan, and China. He has written numerous books and articles on Asia-Pacific management issues and is a frequent speaker on issues related to Asian economics, international management, and global competition. He is a member of EAMSA (Euro Asia Management Studies Association). Dr. Richter's recent publications include *The Dynamics of Japanese Organizations* (Routledge, 1996) and *Business Networks in Asia* (Quorum, 1999).

CONTENTS

Introduction

Since the 1980s, certain management concepts are quoted in an ever-growing literature as being central for the success of Japanese companies: *Total quality control* (TQC), *just-in-time* concepts (JIT), *continuing improvement processes* (CIP), *lean management* and most recently, *reengineering*. In the Western countries, it has become increasingly fashionable to adopt these so-called Japanese management methods. This is done since everything originating in Japan is blindly accepted as efficient and seen as advantageous in competition. Usually the companies are unaware that most of these concepts did not originate in Japan, but instead were developed by American management gurus and are now merely associated with Japanese companies. Managers have been inundated with prescriptions for success. Business books are distilled to a handful of key points or simple models with little room for the vagaries of reality, the inherent messiness of business life.

It is easy to see that misunderstandings and misinterpretations had to evolve in this process. Lean management and reengineering are examples of how supposedly original Japanese management concepts have become the model for the management of companies. Furthermore, these concepts are merely partial concepts and can only partially, if at all, explain the success of Japanese companies.

Lean management became known mostly through *The Machine That Changed the World* by Womack, Jones, and Ross (1990). This book is a detailed and in-depth study of the changed conditions in the development and production of automobiles. Lean management refers to Toyota's extremely efficient and lean production system. However, cost management and waste avoidance have been practiced since Taylor's (1911) economic recommendations. Frederick Taylor, who pioneered what is now known as *scientific management*, separated the planning and design of work from its execution. Taylor expected workers to be as reliable, predictable, and efficient as the

1

robots that are now replacing them. These American or European virtues of efficient economizing had been lost during the years of nearly effortless growth. With the recession of the automobile industry at the end of the 1980s, these lost virtues were rediscovered in Japan and idealized into a myth.

The concept of reengineering tries to dispose of unnecessary efforts and center all processes in the company around the satisfaction of its clients. It tries to reduce production time and achieve total quality. The pioneer book by Hammer and Champy (1993) especially quotes Japanese companies who have successfully implemented reengineering. However, in a near state of euphoria, reengineering as well as lean management have been implemented by American and European companies, while Japanese companies have remained skeptical, probably more aware that such restructuring measures can lead to tightening, entwining, and size adaptation. Such a *downsizing*, correctly identified by Hamel and Prahalad (1994), is not equivalent to an increase in the ability to compete. An increase in productivity through the release of unnecessary overhead is a prerequisite for competitive pricing of products. However, this can possibly limit the creativity potential necessary for the development of new products and the opening up of new markets. Japanese companies are indeed "lean" in their job floor area since the processes in Japan can mostly be standardized and it makes sense to avoid redundancies. Paradoxically, the developmental, administrative, and marketing areas are far from being lean. Generously equipped departments in terms of personnel and overlapping functional areas are more the rule than the exception (Nonaka and Takeuchi, 1995). Western managers who work with efficient informational processing or a reduction of uncertainties will be disturbed by deliberately accepted redundancies. Apparently structures exist in Japanese companies that go beyond the immediate operative needs of employees. These are purposefully overlapping sequences, managerial tasks, and entire organizational units or organizations. The Japanese attitude toward employees emerges here and explains why, despite Japan's current economic difficulties, no downsizings and layoffs have occurred on the scale of those in the United States and Europe.

However, one cannot neglect the economic crisis that is paralyzing Japan in the late 1990s. Almost a decade has passed since the bursting of Japan's "bubble economy"—an era of rampant speculation and sky-high asset price fueled by cheap credit. Yet until recently the nation's economic mandarins have managed to whitewash the severity of the resulting problems, as evidenced by such failed companies as Yamaichi Securities and Hokkaido Takushoku Bank. Instead of focusing on politically difficult reform to ensure long-term economic health, they opted for short-term stability. Sick banks and other companies were maintained by costly life support. Now, with markets jittery from the regional Asian financial crisis, the bill for procrastination has finally come due. However, Japan's top companies—mostly manufacturers—are still on the growth path. While Japan's recession is hurting the banking sector, Japanese blue-chip companies are not worried. Toyota, for instance, is swimming in more than 700 billion yen in cash and other assets quickly convertible into cash, a pile so huge that the car maker scarcely knows what to do with it. In addition to Toyota, many of the names on the Japanese all-star team are familiar—Canon, Honda, Fujitsu. A little-known company, Advantest, has tripled in size over the last three years by becoming the world's largest maker of semiconductor test devices. It is an essential cooperation partner of such giants as Intel and IBM. Advantest manages an array of cooperation agreements both in R&D and marketing with start-up firms and multinationals, with suppliers, customers, and competitors. The biggest contributing factor to Japanese manufacturers' overwhelming success—the hypothesis of this book—is their intelligent approach to interfirm cooperation.

If two or more companies cooperate, redundancies are always created. In an R&D cooperation, for example, the companies usually maintain separate distribution channels to distribute the mutually developed products. In comparison to distribution through a single sales organization, this apparent doubling can finally lead to higher total sales because the cooperating partners are in competition with one another, and have to optimize their production so much, that each individual achieves higher sales. The single companies spur one another on and thus increase their ability to compete.

Japanese companies have institutionalized the organizational redundancy that latently exists in intercompany cooperation actions through *strategic networks*, a system of complex exchange relationships in the vertical and/or horizontal direction (Jarillo, 1988). The so-called *keiretsu* is the most prominent form of strategic network in Japan and spans the industry in a complex relationship arrangement. Mitsubishi, Mitsui, and Sumitomo are firms that represent this practice. A network of dependent companies that encompass important industrial industries such as automobile manufacturers, electronics, and chemical industries gather around a trading firm (*sogo shosha*) and a bank. Aside from the horizontally anchored networks, there are vertically organized networks that form a pyramid-shaped distribution structure. The integrated structure of Toyota is the most famous example of this type of *keiretsu*. In addition to the *keiretsu*, many more types of strategic networks appear in Japan, such as cooperation between companies without *keiretsu* link, start-up companies, or companies with alliances to foreign firms. Kumon and Rosovsky (1992) and Messner (1997) have termed the economic and sociocultural organization of Japan a *network society* to characterize the industrial link and mutual dependency.

Economic success can be linked not only to a company's internal strengths and its ability to continuously achieve production advantages superior to competitors, but also to the way the company handles intracompany relations. Economic relationships are valuable company resources (Hakansson, 1989; Laage-Hellman, 1997; Gemünden, Ritter, and Walter, 1998). The specific layout of the value chain and the linking of companies in Japan is increasingly observed. But the competitive advantage of Japanese companies, for example, in the automobile industries, is not only due to production methods, but explicitly to the supplying organization and quality of the mutual market and technology strategies (Teramoto, 1990; Richter and Wakuta, 1993; Miyashita and Russel, 1994; Dyer, 1996).

Traditional explanations for the building of strategic networks are based on the idea of minimizing transaction costs (Williamson, 1975). This idea evaluates alternative organizational forms—essentially market and hierarchy. The economic activities are organized in such a way as to minimize transaction costs. Networks are an organizational form between market and hierarchy and are a hybrid form of economic actions in relatively unstable environments. This and similar explanations of the idea behind strategic networks, however, tells only part of the story. Increasingly, readily available *knowledge* is responsible for the emergence of strategic networks.

Many companies establish links with other companies in an innovative way, while their knowledge and that of their cooperating partners skips boundaries with increasing speed. The knowledge travels between companies and the boundaries between these are increasingly vanishing (Badaracco, 1991). The ability of companies to learn is essential for the generating of new information. The learning sequences of each cooperative company are linked and a co-evolution of knowledge within a cooperative competition is created. The linking of companies in strategic networks through knowledge is termed *alliance capitalism* (Gerlach, 1992; Cutts, 1992; Dunning, 1997). In this, the Japanese model of an industrial society is based on the original combination of single elements, and thus remains mostly uninfluenced by the economic liberalism of the West as well as by contrasting Marxist ideology. Alliance capitalism is a *capitalism without capitalists* because in strategic networks the interests of those involved must be balanced to maintain stability in the long run. Japan's capitalism differs from that of the Western world. Yoshihara calls the Asian version of capitalism *ersatz capitalism* (Yoshihara, 1988). The Asian capitalists have focused on amassing wealth based on personal contacts and networking, rather than stressing shareholder interests. Understanding the chasm between Western and Eastern versions of capitalism is important now as policymakers and investors debate over globalization. Much of the current discussion centers on mechanics, such as whether it is prudent for Asian countries to reimpose controls on the inflow of foreign currency.

This view is not merely economic rhetoric; hitherto, Japan has had a *sponsored capitalism* controlled by intertwined interest groups. Japanese politicians have recently proposed that individuals and individual firms be allowed to take the initiative. Western opinion has been skeptical (Henderson, 1998), but Japanese observers argue that many influential voices are now emerging in their nation that are no longer willing to toe a monolithic line (e.g., Chikudate, 1995; Tezuka, 1997). Although traditions of internal cooperation are still highly valued, demands for transparency are now strident.

This book does not intend to repeat a description of possible forms of strategic networks as a typical phenomenon of the Japanese culture. Rather it intends to examine the functional mechanisms of strategic networks using Japan as an example. Sugimoto (1997) discards the thesis that the Japanese culture is far more shaped by homogeneity and uniformity than other industrial societies. In many areas of Japan centrifugal forces are at work that are transforming the country into a multicultural society. This is why many phenomena particular to the Japanese economy are also noticeable in other economies. Similar strategic networks exist in Southeast Asia (Weidenbaum and Hughes, 1996; Haley and Haley, 1999) and Korea (Kang, 1997; Shin and Kwon, 1999). Lately, strategic network phenomena are appearing even in China, the so-called *jituangongsi* (Richter, 1997). Overseas Chinese *huarengongsi* in Southeast Asia, Korean *chaebol,* and Chinese *jituangongsi* are similar to the Japanese *keiretsu*, interfirm networks that include companies of different industries and value levels. Strategic networks, however, developed first in Japan. This obviously efficient organizational model was adopted later by other Asian countries and adapted to their particular environments (Chen and Hamilton, 1991).

There are also examples of network organizations in Western industrialized countries, e.g., in California's Silicon Valley (Saxenian, 1990), in Northern Italy (Inzerelli, 1990), in a few parts of Scandinavia (Hadjikhani and Hakansson, 1996) and in Germany (Sydow, 1996). Despite enthusiasm for the success of Japanese companies and the implicit superiority of "Japanese" network cooperation versus "Western" models, one should not forget that strategic network practices are certainly also being employed by Western companies. Only in Japan, however, do networks have such relevance for the economic success of companies, although the latest hit on Japanese companies, one could argue, could speak against Japanese network organizations. The collapse of the *bubble economy* in 1992 and the Asian economic crisis of 1997 onward revealed cracks in Japan's industrial organization. Due to the harsh recession of the last decades and stagnating market shares, Japanese companies are in the process of discarding old recipes of success and searching for new market opportunities. Tselichtchev (1994, 1999) is convinced that the pressure of the current crisis forces Japanese companies to search for more efficient forms of network organizations. While traditional strategic networks were especially oriented toward the home market and intra-*keiretsu* cooperation, ever since the Japanese bubble economy burst in the early 1990s, a stronger orientation toward an internationally spread inter-*keiretsu* cooperation exists.

The first chapter is dedicated to the empirical evidence of intercompany cooperation in Japan and to the theoretical foundation of strategic networks. Aside from a presentation of Japanese network types, strategic networks will be discussed in the context of sociocultural action mechanisms and state intervention. Extreme team spirit in general and the grouping of companies in strategic networks specifically are a typical Japanese model for social relations. The assertiveness of the individual comes from the collectiveness that lends self-respect in exchange for loyalty. The Japanese usually find the warmth and security of belonging to a family through membership and identification in a group. Since the Japanese have such an affinity for the boundaries of group identification, they treat people within and outside of these boundaries differently. Japanese companies pursue, similar to individuals, an extreme focus on the group. Strategic networks are found in all industries and value levels in Japan.

The idea of strategic networks, as developed in this book, is based on a great tradition of thought: Karl Popper's *critical rationalism*. The concepts of *network culture, organizational learning,* and *cooperative competition* in the second chapter are essentially based on Popper's theories (1945; 1963). His theory of critical rationalism, which he views as a method for solving problems, is of great relevance to problems that arise in connection with the shaping and navigating of complex company organizations. Critical rationalism recognizes the possible failure of reason. Any supposed truth can fall prey to a critical examination. All knowledge is thus supposed knowledge; all theories are hypotheses. In strategic networks, companies do not merely exchange knowledge, but question and develop multilevel knowledge components.

In the third chapter, system, growth, and game theories are explained. These can be seen as support constructs for moving toward an understanding of the empirical phenomenon of strategic networks and for describing these networks with the help of explanatory models. It is not our goal, however, to mix ideas in eclectic fashion to describe and differentiate strategic networks. Rather we will try to shed light on single aspects of strategic networks, since none of the ideas satisfactorily explain the structure and dynamic of this complex organizational form. The central goal is to understand the network cooperation in its entirety and multiplicity.

The fourth chapter deals with the ability to work with and navigate within strategic networks. Strategic networks always escape complete control by an individual company, since the network participants usually keep their legal independence. The management of strategic networks is more or less a tautology because the evolution of linked structures cannot be specifically planned or foreseen. Instead, the evolution of such structures works in corrective measures toward a widespread belief that anything is doable. This belief is prevalent in the management of strategic networks. Logistic, technologic, and global cooperation should be understood as examples of a "planned evolution" in the management of strategic networks, which is located between determinism and voluntarism.

The last chapter deals with the demands for a future management coherent with the latent complexity of strategic networks. Beginning with traditional entrepreneurship, the developmental steps to *interpreneurship* are integrated into a new formula of organizational emancipation and discussed. The concept of company size and autocratic control by a manager who is idolized as a doer and hero has lost importance. The organizational form of strategic networks, however, enables the activation of *interpreneurs*, from whom visions and innovations as well as flexible and responsible leadership is expected in smaller and thus more easily comprehensible organizational units. A discussion about the changed demands on economic actions completes the book.

Chapter 1

Japan and Strategic Networks: Site Determination

Whoever writes about the national characteristics of a country's economy and its businesses does so with a bad conscience. Any characterization of a corporation in a national economy is done using generalization, simplification, and sketching and is thus implicitly untrue. Entire businesses cannot be compared to one another using the same standards for all. No single business has all characteristics within its organization that can be attributed to its national economy in its entirety.

At the present time we are far from being a world in which all businesses are the same in the sense that all cultural differences are smoothed out and all businesses are governed by the same cultural values. Probably our world will never achieve such a state. National economies are, like single businesses, distinctive personalities. Exceptions to specific national characteristics can be found within every economic area.

Despite reservations toward generalizations, it cannot be denied that Japanese companies practice behaviors that are very different from those of Western countries. For instance, Japanese companies have a much higher level of "organization" in strategic networks than do their Western counterparts (Ueda, 1986; Teramoto, 1990; Gerlach, 1992; Miyashita and Russel, 1994). European as well as American companies tend to seek out direct competition more often, and until the end of the 1980s only a few entered strategic partnerships. The fact that Japanese companies act differently from their Western counterparts makes this behavior neither better nor worse. We are not proposing that Japanese management methods be transferred to Europe and the United States without reservation.

Unfortunately this was done too often in the past with a sometimes fatal outcome. In the early 1990s, as the lean management and reengineering debates surfaced, many Western companies began rigorous cost management without consideration of already existing agreements. This was done by first horizontally increasing the value chain and then decreasing the number of suppliers. After a period of adaptation, managers of Western companies tried to excuse their setback by pointing to the nontransferability of Japanese methods to Western economies (Yoshihara, 1989; Demes, 1992). The ability of Western companies to use network management is generally denounced by referring to the failure of intercompany cooperation in the electronics and computer industry in such companies as Sematech in the United States or EUREKA in Europe (Lei and Slocum, 1991). Politicians, scientists, and managers nonetheless advise their home companies to acquire strategic networks in order to decrease the apparent disadvantage in comparison to Japan (Ferguson, 1990; Deyer, 1996).

This book will not deal with the advantages and disadvantages of the Japanese model, if there is such a thing. An abundance of information on this topic has been published in the past several years. A separate publication industry has even been established that has originated from the debate of the so-called "Japanese management" (Vogel, 1979; Ouchi, 1981; Abegglen and Stalk, 1987; Van Wolferen, 1989; Fallows, 1994; Anderson and Yoshimura, 1997). Considering the "bubble economy" and the recent Asian financial crisis, others are talking about a new period of corporate development that demystifies Japanese management as currently known (Shimada, 1993; Henderson, 1998). We are neither trying to mythologize Japanese management, nor trying to prophesize an inevitable clash of nations based on the micro- and macroeconomic differences. According to Huntington's view of a "clash of civilizations" (Huntington, 1993), future international debates will be culturally founded. The vanished iron curtain will be replaced by a "velvet curtain" of cultures. The criteria used to distinguish among these cultural areas, will be the history, language, and religion of each individual area. Interestingly, Huntington mentions Japan as being the only country that is equal and isolated in a line of cultural areas among whom future conflicts can arise.

The clash between civilizations and the supposed uniqueness of Japan is now even emphasized by Japan itself. In new-found Japanese confidence, Ishihara pledges for a Japan that "can say no" (Ishihara, 1991) and furthermore for a new pan-Asian self-awareness that is aimed toward rejection of Western principles (Ishihara, 1994). An examination of Japanese strategic networks should be free of those and similar conceptions. Beyond the admiration of Japan's success one can find advice to adopt only selected aspects—such as the cooperation between companies in strategic networks. This attitude is based on the assumption that the entire Japanese model is not entirely positive, is difficult to transfer, and can collide with basic values of the Western countries.

THE CONCEPT OF STRATEGIC NETWORKS

An examination of the literature on networks shows that almost any empirical occurrences in an economic interaction of companies can be regarded as a network. A network is actually no more than a methodical construct of a researcher. First of all, the researcher decides that the research object is registered as a network. Second, the researcher decides how this will be separated by its environment (Nohria, 1992). The constructed research object labeled as a network can be a single business or a group of many companies (Evan, 1965; Aldrich and Whetten, 1981). Perhaps to reflect the empirical diffusion of intermediate modes of coordination, this area of study has suffered from excessive neologism recently. This is not helpful in clarifying how one coined concept relates to another. Depending on the research object and the intention, the connotation of the network can have different attributes. Tichy (1980) discusses *social networks*, Cook and Emerson describe *exchange networks* (Emerson, 1981; Cook and Emerson, 1984), Lincoln (1982) speaks of *inter-organizational networks*, Axelsson and Easton (1992) mention *industrial networks*, Fornengo (1988) depicts *manufacturing networks*, Ueda (1986) describes *intercorporate networks*, Richter (1994) discusses *corporate alliance networks*, Larson (1991) denotes *partner networks*, and finally Hakansson and Snehota (1995) examine *business networks*. Special types of networks are labeled *investment networks* (Bygrave, 1988), *international networks* (Gilroy, 1993), *regional networks* (Sydow, 1996), *market networks* (Baker, 1990), *entrepreneurial networks* (Hansen, 1995), *specialized networks* (Deyer, 1995) and *technological networks* (Gemünden, Ritter, and Heydebreck, 1996). According to the degree of density, multiplexicity, and reciprocity of ties, Achrol even distinguishes among four connotations: *internal market networks, vertical market networks, intermarket networks,* and *concentric networks* (Achrol, 1997). Scher (1997) more specifically refers to networks in Japan as *interfirm networks.*

Jarillo (1988) and Hinterhuber and Levin (1994) refer to a certain type of network that can have the previously mentioned connotations as *strategic networks.* Thus strategic networks differ from other types of networks mostly in that they are strategically guided by one or more focal firms. By strategic, used in conjunction with the term networks, Jarillo means the organization of the network that is guided by economic market demands and technological opportunities (Jarillo, 1988). He regards strategic networks as a mode of organization that can be created by managers to position their firm in a favorable environment. In this framework, the competitive advantage of a firm lies in its capacity to gain access to, and exploit, valued external resources and expertise through the network. This definition most closely fits the network organization of Japanese companies, so that for the rest of this discussion the term strategic networks will refer to these.

According to conventional ideas there are two basic forms of organization of companies within one economic area: one is the internalization of functions in a company, the other is the contract between companies as a buyer and seller in an autonomously defined market. Companies utilizing these two forms have no further dealings beyond their business contract (Williamson, 1975). The possible third form, the intermediary contacts between companies, is of internationally growing importance and also is traditionally important in Japan. Historically, strategic networks have significantly gained importance, especially in the second half of the 1980s. Gilroy (1993) states that a fundamental deficit of theory can be seen in the area of strategic networks. A commonly accepted "network theory" as a closed model for the explanation of the multilayered action mechanisms does not exist.

According to the model of the interaction-oriented network, the market-oriented activities of companies often change to stable interaction relationships (Mattsson, 1987; Hakansson, 1989; Hakansson and Snehota, 1995; Ford et al., 1998). Connections are often regarded as very important resources for the cooperating companies because they allow access to the resources of other network participants. The possibilities for strategic actions of the companies are often determined by their position in the network of the cooperative relationships. This position results from earlier strategic decisions, investments in cooperative relationships, and previous interactions with the cooperative partners.

Teramoto (1990) adds another dimension to this concept: power and dependence between the cooperative partners. He assumes that strategic networks are a self-contained, semistrong organizational unit. Every one of the interacting companies holds or defends a certain position with the goal of receiving further business and resources. The stability of the networks depend on the balance of power within its companies. If the balance of power changes too quickly, the stability of the network will be lost and with it the ability to provide unity.

Gerlach (1992) more specifically looks at the structure of strategic networks through the eyes of an efficient management system: the intra-*keiretsu* relationships of Japan. According to Gerlach, *keiretsu* refers to a web of relationships that usually spans several industries based on mutual and long-term profit increase. The success of the single businesses are very dependent on one another and their strategies can be regarded as complementing one another. In his evaluation and prognosis for success, Gerlach clearly defines *keiretsu* as a web of horizontal and vertical relationships that is separate from the usual agreement between corporations.

Examining the mechanisms of competition necessary for the development of strategic networks can further emphasize the previously named criteria for the interaction, the power, and the structural development of strategic networks. When companies conglomerate to strategic networks they remove themselves from a competitive structure that has been formed by dissociation and hierarchy. According to the traditional rules of competition, companies fight to ensure technological and market-oriented advantages meant to sustain their existence (Porter, 1980). The participants in the market try to improve their own position in comparison to that of their competitors through antagonistic behavior. Furthermore, through diversification they try to nudge into new territories that are not yet occupied by competitors. Diversification occurs through the purchase and takeover of companies as well as through the founding and building up of new organizational units. These often have the character of hostile takeovers and are aimed against competitors. Smaller companies are frequently victims of takeovers by large companies. The original competition then yields to a centrally controlled administration of the acquired and merged companies.

Cooperatives in the traditional order of competition are usually being formed among those suppliers that are in a vertical relationship to the company. These kinds of cooperatives lead to the virtual integration of the suppliers into a production conglomerate led by hierarchy (Richter and Wakuta, 1993). As opposed to a "real" cooperative, the involved parties hereby commit to a relationship of strong dependency. Horizontal cooperatives are usually formed with fast-developing nations. This is done since the laws of those countries usually do not permit a direct investment and instead stipulate the participation of local companies with projects of cooperatives (Rabelloti, 1990). In this case, cooperatives as strategic options do not necessarily meet the global goals of companies.

The scenario of a national economy supported by competition and hierarchy still exists today. However, many companies distance themselves, at least partially, from such stubborn and inflexible structures of competition, and search for cooperatives instead. Companies taking on cooperative agreements previously feared losing control over their own competencies. Now they see strategic networks as a chance to strengthen their own competencies with the cooperatives through mutual stimulation (Ackoff, 1993; Hamel and Prahalad, 1994; Nonaka and Takeuchi, 1995; Lipnack and Stamps, 1996). They realize that their antagonistic behavior results in reduced profit for the companies as a whole and will yield more strategic disadvantages than a cooperative solution. Badaracco (1991) describes an analogy of two different business constellations. One is a medieval fortress that exclusively generates and manages its critical valuables. The other is the Italian city-state of the Renaissance. According to the model of the medieval fortress, the boundaries of the company end at the same point at which its hierarchy ends. The boundaries of the city-state, however, are more variable. The city-states could profit through a fertile exchange with other cities. Mutual trade as well as exchange of art and education gave the city-states a large amount of cultural and economic diversity.

Horizontal cooperation often means that in certain areas and with certain functions, companies cooperate in order to achieve a mutual goal, while maintaining a competitive stance in other areas. Cooperation in the form of strategic networks is being regarded by some authors as the new form of competition. Pucik (1988) and Hamel (1991) refer to this as "competitive collaboration." The character of competition in strategic networks differs from that in hierarchical cooperation through merger and acquisition. The boundaries between friend and enemy are less visible and yield a more ambivalent and very complex entangled relationship structure.

In the early 1980s a unique boom of cooperation between companies started to set in. This was referred to in the literature as "corporate perestroika" (Ackoff, 1993) and was explained by the changes in the competition requirements. Ohmae (1985) and Procassini (1995) argue that using suitable partners is especially useful for companies in a fast-growing industry or for those in need of a reorientation. With "strategic alliance" and "strategic network," a new connotation has even been found for the new type of cooperation. This was done because the classical typology was only able to partially explain the new forms of cooperation between companies in functional areas and legal issues such as joint ventures, licensing agreements, R&D consortia, and others. Many management consultants sold and still sell strategic networks as a management concept of the future (Miles and Snow, 1986; Lei and Slocum, 1991; Jones and Shill, 1991; Salancik, 1995). This trend is reflected in a vast body of publications that recently resulted in a series titled *Studies in Business Organization and Networks* (e.g., Foss, 1997; Colombo, 1998). Publications on Asian networks are particularly popular (e.g., Hamilton, 1991; Gerlach, 1992; Weidenbaum and Hughes, 1996; Fruin, 1998; Richter, 1999). The general mood has probably convinced many hesitant companies that strategic networks are a serious alternative to the classical concept of competition. This might have reinforced a strengthening trend toward cooperative efforts. Imai and Itami (1988) remark that the process by which these types of networks have been formulated is best described as a process of self-organization. The structure that starts to form in a strategic network cannot be planned and predicted in every detail. Imai and Itami regard strategic networks as combining the best of both markets and organizations, maximizing both the flexibility more characteristic of market-oriented transactions and the control more effective within the firm. The development of strategic networks can be presented schematically in comparison to a stable and a changeable environment (see Figure 1.1).

FIGURE 1.1. Behavioral Patterns of Management

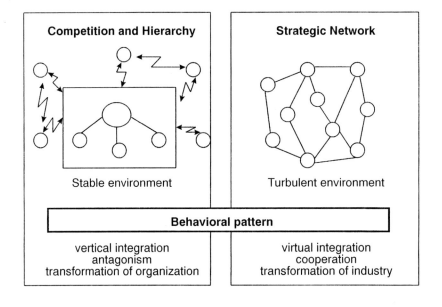

The starting position is determined by competition and hierarchy. The companies use demarcation lines to show the area of their influence and defend these. In a stable environment in which the past can be used to estimate the future, this type of organizational form offers the highest degree of security and greatest ability to plan. When companies enter cooperatives and strategic networks slowly begin to form, then the plannable and controllable environmental levels are left behind and a virtual integration into a changeable environment is sought (Teramoto, 1990). Virtual integration as opposed to vertical integration can be seen as a strategy to form a (possibly only temporary) network of independent companies (Davidow and Malone, 1992; Byrne, 1993; Pasternack and Viscio, 1998). In a virtual, centerless corporation one does without a common institution, a formal organization, or a hierarchy. Firms are built around resources rather than the assets that get lined up on financial balance sheets. They are characterized by the interdependence rather than the independence of their parts. Virtually integrated firms are pancake flat, with a network of interdependent business units and alliances.

The use of strategic networks is characterized by the fact that they can deal with more complex market situations typical for fast-growing industries. One can no longer passively react to environmental influences by being more closed off. The newfound flexibility can much better be used to consciously influence the corporate environment (Drucker, 1980). Depending on the interest and the circumstances, new cooperations can be formed, and old ones can be dissolved or defined in a new way.

In the classic arena of industrial activity, competition is an antagonistic behavior directed on economies of scale. In contrast, competition as a cooperative means that competition coexists with a cooperative in strategic networks. The cooperation in strategic networks can either extend to just one or a few functional areas, leaving the companies in competition in other functional areas. The relationship between the cooperative partners can change further over time. Corporate relationships that originally existed with a common interest can shift to competitive relationships (Hamel, 1991; Teramoto, Richter, and Iwasaki, 1993). Erratic directional changes can be observed especially among high-tech companies.

The current existing pressure on many companies to change their organization by utilizing reengineering, lean management, downsizing, and other methods is often due to the fact that in the past these companies missed becoming part of a strategic network and thus have missed the change in the industrial arena. In conceptualizing structures of competition, Porter (1980) aimed at the change and adaptation of internal organizational structures in any given industrial area. He thereby greatly negated the implicit possibility of an industrial change through an integration of overlapping businesses in strategic networks. A successfully completed organizational change can make a company lean and flexible. In their book *Competing for the Future,* Hamel and Prahalad show that, through a change, a lean company does not automatically ascend to being a pioneer company in a certain industrial segment. It is not necessarily capable of forming new segments through the combination of existing ones (Hamel and Prahalad, 1994). To set a precedent, a company has to personally take the process of industrial change into its own hands and has to define the rules of the political alliance within the strategic networks.

Companies that have recognized the heightened complexity of economizing are starting to ease themselves out of the old order of competition. This order, which has proven effective under the circumstances of moderate complexity, is no longer sufficient and does not necessarily lead to the goal (Grant, 1996; Davis and Meyer, 1997). The trouble is that the connections are so numerous and so complex that they can bring things to a grinding, inexplicable halt. Myriad connections are speeding up the economy and, more critically, changing the way it works.

Those companies that continue trying to reduce complexity in the traditional way are drifting into chaos and will possibly have to fear for their survival. Kanter (1982) associates this with the anachronism of many multinational companies and asks for a reconsideration of companies' strategies. When complex economics have become too large to sufficiently filter the flood of information coming from all the companies, the organization has to be restructured in such a way that it can manage itself from the outside and can supply itself proactively with knowledge.

Because of the development of strategic networks, the economic theory needs indicators other than market shares, turnover, employment numbers, or capital assets of individual companies to determine the competitive advantages. The prospect of strategic networks which allow access to knowledge resources, explains the desire of companies to enter into cooperative agreements. Japanese companies, as we will show, are masters in the opening and development of knowledge through a proactive management of strategic networks. In the next section we will try to illustrate and discuss the empirical relevance of strategic networks in Japan. Networks have existed long before the network euphoria that started growing in the Western countries. This might be one reason why strategic networks are considered typically Japanese.

EMPIRICAL EVIDENCE
FOR STRATEGIC NETWORKS IN JAPAN

In Japan, stockholders have no real power over companies—many yearly stockholder meetings last less than an hour. To keep potential critics from talking during the meetings, a branch of organized crime—the so-called *sokaiya*—has offered its services until recently. Although these strategies are being fought more fiercely, it is still not foreseeable that the individual stockholder can have substantial influence in the near future (Reading, 1992; Wood, 1992; Miyashita and Russel, 1994).

The important mechanism of company control lies in the combination of companies in the network (Gerlach, 1992). A first controlling factor stems from the fact that Japan's companies traditionally are highly dependent on outside capital assets. This capital is made available through financial intermediaries, especially banks. Many companies, even large ones, have a house bank that takes care of most loans and monitors the performance of the companies. The supervision is not focused on the daily financial activities, but instead is more effective in a crisis situation. Another controlling factor lies in the interconnection of the companies among each other, especially in the form of alternating capital shares (Ueda, 1991). In view of Japan's sociocultural setting, this fosters the establishment of mutual trust. Influence on the basis of such interweaving of capital is usually indirect and not exercised in public meetings.

In order to strengthen the *uchi*, which is the companies' community balancing the influence of capital, stocks, which are the property of the actual company, are primarily sold to befriended companies. The term "befriended" companies refers to those that are connected to each other through the network cooperative. These companies have the interest to make decisions to the advantages of their cooperative. Sixty to seventy percent of all Japanese companies' stocks are spread through mutual involvement in such a way as to protect the companies' groups from almost any hostile measure, force compromises, and maintain the stability. It is no coincidence then, that cooperating companies in Japan are interwoven through mutual assets. It stems from the priority that *uchi* takes over *soto*, the stranger that is inherently seen in a threatening and compressing role. This priority could no longer be upheld if the company were to fall into just anyone's hands. Strangers have no commitment toward the employees of a company. They have to be kept at a distance because they could decide in the best short-term interest and could thwart the long-term interests of the group.

A further controlling factor is contained in the tight link between the economy and politics, the so-called "administrative guidance." The economic-political process is essentially formed by the government and parliament, by the federal government, the ministerial bureaucracy especially, the private companies with their associations, and finally by the employers and their representatives. Japanese economic politics have been characterized over a period of several decades by a symbiosis of the higher bureaucracy in the ministry, by the politicians of the reigning Liberal Democratic Party (LDP), and by the private companies bound into strategic networks. The slogan *Japan Inc.*, which can only partially describe the complex economic political relationship in Japan, arose from the tight link between these authorities. The *keiretsu* as a flagship of the Japanese economy is bound into a social system of mutual dependency. Strategic networks in Japan are part of an economic system that has stabilized in its own rationality. On the basis of organizational learning and constant adaptation, developments and structures started to form that fit well into these adaptations. An important motivation is the cooperative competition within and between the *keiretsu* that constantly forces the companies into adaptation.

Japanese Network Types

The types of strategic networks found in Japan today have a substantial part of their historical roots in the tightly run *zaibatsu*, which are conglomerates with family-owned companies at the top. The development of the *zaibatsu* to the *keiretsu* as an interwoven organization made up of independent companies can be traced back to economic reforms that occurred between the world wars and especially following World War II (Aoki, 1988; Morikawa, 1992). Prior to this, during the period of national isolation in the Tokugawa period (1603-1868) a Confucian class order was established. This order first made up the basis for free trade and later, with the beginning of the Meiji reforms, it served as the basis for the industrial revolution.

Two Sino-Japanese characters (*kanji*), combine in *keiretsu*. Separately the meanings are *kei*: system, stem, line, clique, connection; and *retsu*: row, line, link. The historical meaning is translated as "relationship of things arranged according to a certain lawfulness" (Miyashita and Russel, 1994). The importance that strategic networks have reached in Japan must be understood with these laws in mind, and they will need to be discussed in further detail. The development of strategic networks was made easier only through historical developments and socioeconomic conditions. At the same time they were stabilized by these developments. Today three types of strategic networks exist: capital *keiretsu*, production *keiretsu*, and trans-*keiretsu* (see Figure 1.2).

Probably the most famous type of Japanese network is the horizontally organized capital *keiretsu* (Japanese: *kinyu keiretsu*, also *kigyo shudan*: corporate group). The six large firms Mitsubishi, Mitsui, Sumitomo, Sanwa, Fuyo, and Daiichi Kangyo, the *rokudai kigyo shudan* (see Yoshinari, 1992) can be assigned to this type of network. Firms of various sizes and trades that are cross-linked through capital investments, group around one bank and one trading firm (Young, 1979; Hiroshi, 1991; Gerlach, 1992). The linking of capital investments protects the firms from hostile takeovers and ensures equal growth for all organized firms within the *keiretsu*.

Gerlach's (1992) in-depth study of leading Japanese capital *keiretsu* showed intergroup borrowing ranged from over 42 percent for

FIGURE 1.2. Japanese Network Types

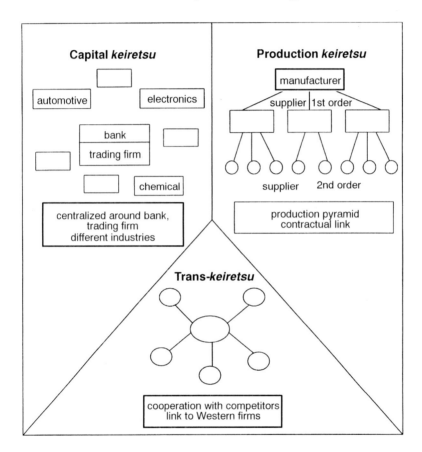

the Mitsubishi and Sumitomo groups to a low of 23 percent for Daiichi Kangyo group firms. The Mitsubishi and Sumitomo groups also reveal the highest levels of intergroup crossholding of equity capital at over 63 percent, the lowest being 28 percent in the Sanwa group.

The presidents of the member companies of a capital *keiretsu* regularly hold meetings in which they discuss the politics of the group. The basis of this *kai* is the alternatingly held stock of the firm. The *kai* aids the integration to the inside and the symbolism to the outside of the internal network boundaries. For example, the *nimokukai* (second-Thursday meeting), is the roundtable for the Mitsui-*keiretsu*, at which the presidents of about 30 firms meet (Miyashita and Russel, 1994). The chairmanship of this institution changes regularly between Mitsui Corporation (trading firm), Sakura Ginko (bank) and Mitsui Real Estate. Gerlach (1992) observes that the atmosphere is one of camaraderie rather than a formal meeting with a defined agenda. Hence, the horizontal layers of interfirm councils serve more of a sociocultural purpose than an economic one. They function less as a means of command and control for determining the policies and practices of individual companies and more as a forum for discussion of matters of mutual concern.

The firms' bank that makes up the center of a capital *keiretsu* together with the trading firm (e.g., Sumitomo Bank, Fuji Bank) takes over the financial operations for the rest of the firms. The bank, in addition to covering the typically large outside financial need of Japanese firms, also conveys business to the *keiretsu* members and supports them with strategic advice. In the event that one member firm is in need of a capital increase, the other firms in the network can possibly provide the capital by reorganizing the capital share.

The firms usually supply each other with goods and services while the *sogo shosha* (trading companies) together with the banks make up the center of the group. They promote the mediation among the firms of a group as well as assume the gathering of information and the project planning. The *sogo shosha* function in some, but not in all six large *keiretsu* as the strategic center and control and in the planning and development of resources. Until the mid-1970s the *sogo shosha* exported 70 percent of Japan's iron, steel, and machinery products, and accounted for nearly half its machinery imports (Gerlach, 1992). Furthermore, under the guidance of the *sogo shosha,* the establishment of a new firm can be made on the basis of mutual investments of the groups' companies, thus further strengthening the new firm's potential and cohesion. The main job of the *sogo shosha* is the development and maintenance of interorganizational relationships.

Mitsubishi, Mitsui, and Sumitomo are tightly internally interwoven, well-organized firms. These three capital *keiretsu* originated directly from the so-called prewar *zaibatsu*, large autocratically led conglomerates that were managed by one family (Okumura, 1981; Morikawa, 1992; Hoshi, 1994). The *zaibatsu* had a strong economic position, as well as an indirectly strong political position. In 1945, the administration of the occupying forces of the United States viewed the *zaibatsu* and its representing concentration of power as one of the reasons for the military expansion of Japan. For this reason its breakdown was attempted. However, the United States had carried out a restructuring policy in an effort to contain communism in the late 1940s. Thus, they were now interested in a capitalistically strong Japan, and a new concentration was not prevented. However, the original companies of the *zaibatsu* were dissolved and the stocks that were in the possession of the families were released. With this, the families lost their power over the attached companies. Today Mitsubishi, Mitsui, and Sumitomo, aside from being associated with the firms whose *keiretsu*-affiliation can be recognized by its name (e.g., Mitsubishi Motors, Mitsui Bank, Sumitomo Chemical), encompass firms such as Asahi Glass and Kirin (Mitsubishi-*keiretsu*), Toyota and Toshiba (Mitsui-*keiretsu*) as well as NEC and Matsushita (Sumitomo-*keiretsu*).

As opposed to the firms that directly evolved from the successor organization of the *keiretsu*, the other large capital *keiretsu* Sanwa, Daiichi Kangyo, and Fuyo arose out of the necessity of the postwar years to restructure and economically consolidate. They are more informally organized and are more often connected to independent large firms and smaller groups. The Fuyo-*keiretsu* is largely comprised of undissolved firms of the Yasuda-*zaibatsu*, one of the prominent *zaibatsu* of the prewar period. Thus the Fuji Bank, the previous Yasuda-Bank, forms the center of the Fuyo-*keiretsu*. Other firms such as Nissan, Canon, and NKK sided with dissolved *zaibatsu* that did not own their own bank. The Sanwa-*keiretsu* is especially regionally concentrated in the Kansai area (around Osaka, Kobe, and Kyoto) and includes firms such as Kobe Steel, Daihatsu, and Sharp. The Daiichi-*keiretsu* is the youngest of the six large *keiretsu*. It emerged in 1971 from the merger of two banks, Daiichi Ginko and Nippon Kangyo Ginko. The respective connections such as Shiseido, Isuzu, and Fujitsu were introduced.

In the production *keiretsu* (in Japanese: *seisan keiretsu* or *kigyo keiretsu*), several supply firms are grouped around one goods investment industry firm along the value chain. They are subcontractors to the manufacturing firm. They can be found especially in those industries which are multifaceted (mechanical engineering, vehicle manufacturing, electronics, and precision engineering industry). The economic independence of these firms is greatly restricted since they exclusively produce for one or two buyers at the most (Cole and Yakushiji, 1984; Demes, 1992). Such subcontract relationships lead to an interwoven production and delivery structure. The most famous example for a production *keiretsu* is the integrated structure of Toyota.

In the Japanese automobile industry, the supplier firms take on a special role. Their job is mainly to manufacture parts, components, or provide services for one or more automobile companies. The economic relationship between automobile manufacturers and supplier firms is that of a vertical cooperation in the entire manufacturing process. The automobile manufacturer is self-limited to the planning, development, and manufacturing of a few elements of the final product as well as the final assembly. The supplying firms are entrusted with the manufacturing of all components and are responsible for the pre-assembly. The supplying firms in turn have smaller partner firms provide parts and components so that the production structure takes on the form of a pyramid.

The supplying firms are strongly bound to the automobile firms. The economic relationships usually have exclusive rights, so that firms such as Toyota and Nissan can rely on relatively stable production structures. The economic dependency of the supplying firms is great in comparison, since they conclude about two-thirds of their turnover with one automobile firm. The exclusiveness of this relationship, however, limits the operational radius of the suppliers. They have to accept limitations in the free structuring of the work processes and in the setting of the price, but have to only partially act market oriented. Japanese automobile firms draw sales contracts with the suppliers over the entire production time of a model and usually renew these for the follow-up model. The contracts however do not specify the exact purchasing quantity and the price. The suppliers commit to price adjustments when demanded rationalization efforts have to be pushed through.

The close relationship between suppliers and automobile firms can further be seen in the fact that the automobile firms advise and support the suppliers in technical, financial, and personal matters. The automobile firms expect their suppliers to deliver just-in-time and to continually improve their manufacturing process. In times of crises, constant pressure is exerted to decrease costs and thereby prices. For this reason Japan's economy is referred to as a "dual economy" because of its vertical cooperation (Helper and Levine, 1992).

The Japanese economy is structurally segmented into large capital asset-intensive companies with a high level of job security and into peripheral subcontract companies with a low level of job security. According to Takamura (1991) and Odagiri (1992), the existence of a dual economy has a functional origin in the effective cost management along the value chain as well as a historical origin. In contrast to Western firms, Japanese firms hesitated in the postwar years to vertically integrate because of chronic lack of capital as well as to avoid taking risks.

A further type of strategic network in Japan is a trans-*keiretsu*. Strategic networks are not only limited to the classical connections within the capital and production *keiretsu*, but also stretch beyond the *keiretsu*-boundaries as cooperations with firms of other *keiretsu*, with *keiretsu*-free Japanese firms, or with foreign firms. Furthermore, cooperations form in Japan between start-up firms that do not have the necessary assets for a vertical integration and have to therefore limit themselves to the center activities. The necessary strategic resources are being supplied through cooperation agreements.

In this sense, trans-*keiretsu* can be seen as a connection between the *keiretsu*. On the other hand, they introduce new units into the game. An interesting example is the networking of NTT, the largest and former state-owned Japanese telecommunication firm, with the most important Japanese telecommunication and electronics firms such as NEC, Fujitsu, Hitatchi, and Toshiba. NTT gives development contracts to these companies that, as competitors, are very similar to each other in their abilities and structures, but that under the guidance of NTT join together in mutual development projects and even production joint ventures. This so-called *NTT family* (Teramoto, 1990) constitutes a complex net of relationships of both cooperative as well as competitive nature.

Often single firms are part of a production—as well as capital *keiretsu*. Toyota, for example, is in the Mitsui-*keiretsu*, and because of shares with Daihatsu is bound into the Sanwa-*keiretsu*. However, it has its own production *keiretsu* with the firm leading it at its disposal. Toyota holds many shares, some with firms such as Chiyoda Fire and Towa Real Estate. As the largest single firm in Japan, Toyota continually keeps increasing its shares with firms that are only indirectly linked to the automobile industry. However, Toyota rarely acquires a firm totally, but instead holds only minority shares (Miyashita and Russel, 1994). From this perspective, Toyota is a capital *keiretsu* that only lacks the size and the function of a bank in order to be able to join the six large *keiretsu*. Indeed financial business is done using either the Sakura Bank (Mitsui-*keiretsu*) or using the Tokai Bank, a local bank in Toyota's home country prefecture Aichi. Recently, Toyota is even helping bail out Tokai Bank which has been affected by the Japanese "bubble economy" and the current Asian financial crisis. Toyota directly as well as indirectly has the relative majority of the Tokai Bank, so that the Toyota-group—group referring to the entirety of the maintained cooperations on all levels—may be portrayed as a hybrid form between capital and production *keiretsu* and as a nexus between different capital *keiretsu* (Mitsui and Sanwa). The picture is being complemented with several foreign cooperational agreements such as GM and Volkswagen.

In the past few years a certain turning away from the relatively solidly placed structures of the capital and production *keiretsu* can be seen, since they can restrict the entrepreneurial flexibility as is periodically argued (Richter and Wakuta, 1993; Tselichtchev, 1994; Liebeskind et al., 1996; Deyer, 1996). Firms are increasingly entering cooperation agreements with firms outside of their own *keiretsu*. In the mid-1990s, for example, the three Japanese truck manufacturers came together to develop axle systems together. Even among the medium-sized firms the strategy to work together in networks finds great approval. In so-called *igyoushu koryu* (networks for technological activities, see: Furukawa, 1985; Stam, 1992) start-up companies come together to complement one another with project-specific parts of the value chain.

Another amazing example of trans-*keiretsu* is the *amoeba* system of Kyocera Corporation (Zeleny, 1990). The *amoeba* are independent, profit-sharing, and self-responsible units within the network of intracorporate relationships. Each *amoeba* carries out its own planning, profit system, cost accounting, and human resource management. They compete, subcontract, and cooperate among themselves on the basis of the intracompany market of market-derived transfer prices. Depending on demand and amount of work, *amoebas* can divide into smaller units. They are authorized to trade intermediate products with outside companies; if the internal supplier is unreasonable, the buyer *amoeba* will search for a satisfactory supplier outside the company. This system represents quite a revolutionary step beyond the traditional production *keiretsu*.

Since the end of the 1980s the trans-*keiretsu* supplement the traditional forms of interfirm cooperation. Trans-*keiretsu* are fundamentally more flexible. Temporary commitments can be dissolved when the market emphasis shifts. Whether capital *keiretsu*, production *keiretsu*, or trans-*keiretsu*, the phenomenon of strategic networks has enormous relevance in Japan. However, some analysts believe that the keiretsu system has seen its zenith in the boom years of the 1980s (Shimada, 1993; Chikudate, 1995; Tselichtchev, 1999). Certainly Japan's persistent recession has caused loosening of network density and strained the "family values" of the system. The percentage of shares on the Tokyo stock exchange held in stable intercorporate investments has dropped from 71 percent in 1988 to 65 percent in 1994. The inroads made by independent discount retailers have affected relations with the multitiered distribution networks of small stores affiliated with the *keiretsu*. Small store share of retail sales has dropped from 35 percent in 1982 to 25 percent in 1994. And critical values such as lifetime employment and loyalty to suppliers have been shaken.

Uchi-Soto *in the Japanese Society*

The astonishing flexibility of Japanese companies that is evident in the naturalness with which Japanese companies enter into network cooperations must be viewed in connection with the group orientation of the employees. The single employee usually does not follow an abstract principle, long or short term. Abstract rules are hardly necessary since individual space cannot be fenced off or harmonized. The constant dialogue with the comrade-in-arms about the correct way is crucial. Therefore, different rules apply in the group (*uchi*) than on the outside (*soto*). With this, the actual attitude toward something has to be differentiated from the position represented by the outside (Kuwayama, 1992). The contrast between *uchi* and *soto* can be seen as the underlying social principle that is hidden behind the phenomenon of strategic networks. The companies within the network see themselves as *uchi*, while companies outside of the network are being seen as *soto*, and thus as a latent threat to the internal structure of a network.

According to the concept of Nakane (1970), Japanese society is organically and vertically organized. Affiliation with a certain group (family, village, company) is much more important to behavior than the horizontal connections concerning a certain type of education, for example. Abstract rules of conduct play almost no role. It is much more important that the members conduct themselves in a loyal fashion. The basic model for this relationship pattern is *ie*, the family. Conflicts are resolved on the inside; *ie* is planned for the long term. The present members see themselves only as a part in the line of ancestors and following generations. Mitsui, for example, was successful with a firm policy based on this attitude from the early nineteenth century and successfully led 1,000 employees (Gerlach, 1992).

The necessity and desire to live in groups was already established with the introduction of the rice culture in primitive Japanese history. The cultivation of rice requires large quantities of water, making extensive and complicated irrigation systems necessary in mountainous Japan. The installation of rice terraces on the steep slopes is arduous, strenuous, and requires the assistance of every able village member. They also have to work together precisely and in tune with one another. If a rice terrace is not exactly cut horizontally into the hill then it cannot be irrigated properly. Just as important is the continual distribution of water and the maintenance of the canals and sluices. The cultivation of rice forces a village into a continuous mutual effort; everyone helps one another. Following this period, an agrarian society with relatively little differentiation was formed (Kitaro, 1987). In contrast, ancestors from Western civilizations were hunters whose courage and skill rewarded each individual.

The traditional Japanese house is still used today by the majority of the population and leaves little room for privacy. Walls of thin wood allow any sound to be heard outside. Since the small houses are crowded closely together due to the limited space, the entire neighborhood hears every loud word. Until recently, Japanese entrance doors remained unlocked. There was no one to lock them against. Strangers did not enter the village, and if they did, they were recognized as such immediately, and since everyone was part of a large community there was nothing to hide from one another.

In the traditional Japanese society the smallest *uchi*-unit was the family, the next higher one was the extended family, then a village, a prefecture, and the nation. The boundaries that constitute *uchi* can then be shifted to the inside or outside. As if changing perspectives, concentric rings form around the observed *uchi*-unit (Berque, 1992). The possibility of shifting boundaries differentiates the Japanese *uchi*-concept from the philosophical tradition of its Asian neighbors, China and Korea, who exhibit stronger individuality and relation to one's own family (Chinese: *jia*, Korean: *taek*). The flexibility of the boundaries between *uchi* and *soto* often play a big role in the preservation of social integrity and the avoidance of conflicts. Berque (1992) stresses that whereas European cultures have tended to give the individual a stable, central, or even transcendental position, Japanese culture tends to give the individual a relative position. In Figure 1.3, an *uchi*-unit is marked, whereby the companies, symbolically illustrated as circles are *uchi* themselves. In the context of a strategic network, the surroundings of a company are connected and widened to an all-encircling *uchi*.

An employee of a large Japanese company almost inevitably develops a team spirit within the department or the profit center in which he works. Possibly two departments are competing for the

FIGURE 1.3. *Uchi* and *Soto* in the Economic Context

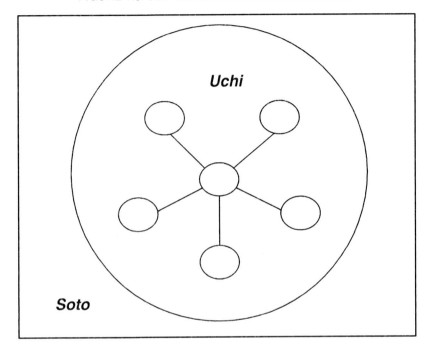

same resources during the budgeting. The employees will do what-ever they can for the interests of their respective department, since they perceive themselves as being connected with the *uchi*. This attachment developed through a long process of socialization and refers to the dependency of the employee on the immediate field of work. *Nomunication* (Japanese: *nomu*: to drink, and English: com-munication) are unofficial meetings that take place at the end of the work day with the goal of building a mutual group identity and thereby an *uchi*. The colleagues of a department mutually drink *sake* in one of the many bars (*izakaya*) specialized for these groups of people, and thus they grow closer to each other by sharing expe-riences and worries.

The next largest *uchi* unit is the company itself. With the begin-ning of industrialization, the traditional *uchi* units of family and village were replaced by companies as the most important social group. New employees are usually not hired for a specific task, as is customary in Western countries. Instead, the employee introduces himself unrestricted and open-minded to a company and leaves it up to the company to choose the exact field of work for him. The graduate of a university does not apply for a specific job, but instead applies to belong to a certain company in general. Most Japanese answer the question about their line of work not by stating their job, but instead saying that they work "for Toyota" or "with Mitsubishi." Lifelong employment is rewarded to those who commit themselves unconditionally to a large company. The company offers much more than just job fulfillment. As a modern patriarch, it takes over the role of the extended family. The employees often spend their vacation in a company-owned vacation home, although it is usually not customary to use up all the vacation time, documenting that work is taken more seriously than leisure time. It is no rarity that bosses try to set up the single men of a company with suitable women (*omiai*). Of course they are also sought within their own companies, since a wife who once worked in a company has a special understanding for the duties of an employee in working long hours and not using vacation time. In this way a Japanese company is portrayed as a sort of "community of fate" (Doi, 1986; Dore, 1994; Goldman, 1994; Sai, 1995). The workforce of many large companies starts the day by singing the company's own anthem. Thus it is logical to see the company as an *uchi* and a modern replacement of the *ie*.

Aside from the center of *uchi* as identification with the individual company, the boundaries to group feeling can be extended. The companies gather as groups in strategic networks and develop a behavioral codex valid for all companies in the network. This is why the Mitsubishi-*keiretsu* possibly has other ideas about *uchi* than does the Fuyo-*keiretsu*. The companies in the Toyota production alliance distance themselves from the suppliers for Nissan. The affiliation with a company group can especially be seen in the staffing policies (Odagiri, 1992). In times of supply or demand surplus, permanent staff can be loaned to befriended companies (*shukko*). The strategic resources of the companies can be relatively freely shifted within the boundaries of the strategic network.

Even if Japanese companies enter a cooperative agreement with foreign companies, these become integrated into the *uchi* of the

Japanese side. The companies mutually become one anothers' environment, if the foreign company does not mind the "possession," and interact in such a way that only structural changes which do not jeopardize their own existence are undertaken. The individual development of a company is coupled with that of another company and the interactions mesh with each other.

In Japan, the individual is available for the group and is also dependent on it. The individual lives and works for the group. All other relationships are vague and hold more responsibilities than rights (Berque, 1992). Due to this very close relationship the state has assumed few social security contributions. Most likely the groups are not greatly interested in having the state take over the duties. They do not want to jeopardize the loyalty that every individual has toward them by making a foreign authority such as the state the point of reference. The welfare provided by the group is not considered charity because as a loyal member of the group, every person has a right to receive help. A mentality that allows an individual to burn all bridges behind him, hoping that the state keeps him alive, is unthinkable under these circumstances.

Certainly groups, alliances, and networks can be found all over the world, but nowhere do they play such an important role as a naturally developed, unconditionally accepted social organization. This Japanese lifestyle has nothing to do with a forced merger, or with collectives of totalitarian systems, because this is a place in which people feel secure, not suppressed. Japanese groups usually are not ordered around, but instead normally make their decisions in a democratic way. The Japanese lifestyle is a product of its own history.

Administrative Guidance

In Japan, economic decisions are often made without public involvement. This is true for decisions between companies as well as for those made by the government that pertain to industry. Since the agreements are based on long-standing personal contacts, there is no need to formalize them. A social system made up of ex-presidents, company bosses, and former government employees is hidden behind the so-called "old boy's network." These individuals serve as advisors on political and economic committees. There are appropriate channels for these types of arrangements because it is customary in Japan for high-ranking government officials, especially those from the department of finance, to take over high positions in the industry after leaving active duty (*amakudari*: to descend from one's height). These government officials link the goals of the state bureaucracy with those of the industry.

The state and the economic system are connected to each other in a symbiotic relationship. The economic system is not completely free from state intervention. It is responsible for paying taxes and contributing to the financing of the state and is under state supervision in regard to the public order. The state's tie is not direct, but rather an indirect control which is referred to in Japan as "administrative guidance" (*gyosei shido*) (Gilroy, 1993).

The roots of administrative guidance can be found in the Meiji Restoration (1868-1912). With the reintroduction of the emperor (*tenno*) as the central political power and the opening of the country to the West, one of the important goals was the establishment of an economic structure that included a bank and monetary system, postal and transportation system, heavy industry, etc. Companies and industries that were determined indispensable for the establishment of a strong nation were supported (Morikawa, 1992). Those sectors that were thought to be too risky by Japanese investors or those that faced huge starting difficulties were supported by the state itself. Later, the families at the top of a *zaibatsu* awarded financial help in political and military expenses to the government. This granted them protection and in return—out of a feeling of obligation—the industrials lent them an open ear.

In the administrative guidance, three different partners are involved: the ministerial bureaucracy, the Liberal Democratic Party (LDP), and the *keiretsu* (see Figure 1.4). The *keiretsu*, which profit from the pursuit of a political course of growth through the ministries and the LDP financially, support elections with campaign donations and do not substantially resist their political influence. Thus one speaks in Japan of a "symbiotic triangle" (Johnson, 1993).

As with a tripod, every leg is equally important for the stability of the structure in the administrative guidance. Politics gives a relatively large leeway as long as economic politics, which encourages growth, is sought. It establishes a general satisfaction among the

FIGURE 1.4. Administrative Guidance

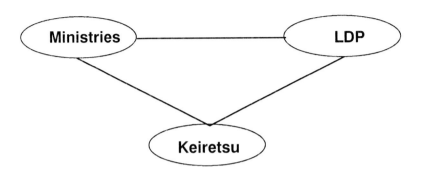

voting population and allows for special allocations to the voters of the LDP, especially the rural population. Thus the position of the administrative vice minister is often stronger than those of the often-changing ministers. Japan's conservative parties and governments have never looked upon the financing of politics through industry as a blemish. They do not view politics and economics as separate entities with opposite interests but instead view them as natural partners of an interest group.

Next to the three elements of the symbiotic triangle of *keiretsu*, LDP, and government, business associations such as Keidanren, Nikkeiren, Nisho, and others play a decisive role. One of the main functions of the associations is to serve as an intermediary between the *keiretsu* companies, the government, and the LDP. The political influence of the associations is most apparent in economic politics with its important areas of the industrial structure, the finance, income, and social politics (Hollerman, 1988). The support of the LDP appears to be the ideal way for the associations to secure the continuity of their basic requirements and the political order.

The close relationship between administration and economy is often regarded as negative by Western countries and is branded by terms such as "Japan Inc." The most important source for this view as the "revisionists" Hoyt (1991), Johnson (1993), Bartu (1992), and Hall (1998) claim, is the supposed conspiratory system of the

Japanese economy. It harmed the established industrial nations of the West and could only be halted through political pressure. To the West the interaction between administration and economy appears as a felting of the political system, as the indirect tax mechanisms are hard to follow. As Hall (1998) notes, a great deal is at stake for the rest of the world if Japan continues to selectively include and systematically exclude foreigners. This becomes all too clear in the derogatory term, Japan Inc. Whereas Hall sees Japan as a monolith that responds only to pressure, Katz (1998) is more skeptical and realistic. He contends that when the American revisionists influenced the policy of the first two years of the Clinton administration, the policy backfired. Japan became, if anything, even more intransigent. This Western attitude toward Japan has a long tradition. Ever since Commodore Matthew Perry's ships arrived in 1853 to force feudal Japan to open up to the West, *gaiatsu*—foreign pressure—has played a pivotal role in shaping Japanese policy.

The *keiretsu* are obviously seen as an organizational form for pushing through their own interests in the Japanese socioeconomic environment. This happens at the cost of outsiders, especially the non-Japanese competitors. Foreign companies have difficulty establishing themselves on the Japanese market (Van Wolferen, 1989; Teramoto et al., 1994; Lasserre and Schütte, 1995). The connections between the Japanese companies appear too complex and nontransparent and seem to leave the foreigners out in the cold. The impenetrability of Japan Inc. does not necessarily have to be seen as a conscious blockade toward foreigners. Yet indeed, *keiretsu* are the gatekeepers. One has to be an insider—*uchi*—to successfully enter the market.

The Japanese distribution system is an immense entrance barrier. The need for a new competitor to secure the distribution and sale of a product opens the possibility of erecting market entrance barriers through the distribution system (Van Wolferen, 1989; Czinkota and Woronoff, 1991; Kikuchi, 1995). Quite unlike the American market, the critical variable for reaching the Japanese consumer is the ability to properly tap the distribution network. In addition, formal import regulations, though transparent, are often onerous and discourage entry into the Japanese market. Yet, opaque administrative practices are more troubling. The Japanese bureaucracy can reject import shipments without even having to explain to the shipper the basis for this rejection. The more limited the large and small business channels for a product, and the more such a product is dependent on established competitors, the more difficult it is to enter the market. The relationships between manufacturer and distributor are personal and require stability and loyalty. These are attributes that a foreign company must first establish.

Extreme competition occurs between Japanese companies with similar product portfolios. This competition is supported by the government insofar as it seems useful for the entire country. As soon as it could harm the country, the state bureaucracy intervenes by limiting competition or by directing it toward mutual goals (Fransman, 1990; Takeda, 1991). Probably the most legendary image among the state authorities is that of the MITI (Ministry of International Trade and Industry), which is mostly responsible for the manufacturing industry and parts of the tertiary sectors. The vertically arranged departments in the MITI that are responsible for individual industries must be distinguished from the horizontally arranged departments with their responsibilities for the foreign trade of the entire nation. The vertical departments often see themselves as representatives of their interests and keep in very close contact with private economy. They design future scenarios for the industries that mainly focus on problems, sketch out solutions, show prioritizing measurements, and set goals and useful guidelines. These plans have no executing power. However, they are based on such a broad understanding of the economy that the general course of action for the next years can be determined accordingly. The scenarios can certainly be regarded as sketches for future strategies. However, they should not be misinterpreted as the script for a closed unified nation (Hollerman, 1988; Okimoto, 1989). These scenarios promote communication within the symbiotic triangle and they strengthen the trust of large parts of the population by successfully coping with future challenges.

The existence of various organizational structures in the Japanese economy gives the MITI numerous levers, or points of access, to intervene in the marketplace. In the same vein, bureaucratic power is also relational because it emerges from the structure of bureaucracy-interest group alignments and the political exchanges that take place among them. The secret to the power of the Japanese state is thus embedded in the structure of its relationship to the rest of society. Japan is without question a network society.

The 1990s have been a dismal decade for Japan. It has gone from being the fastest-growing economy among the industrialized nations to being mired in a homegrown recession with real gross domestic product (GDP) growing by an average of only 0.5 percent over the 1991 to 1998 period. The MITI's disastrous decisions of wasting enormous sums by targeting an analog-based, high-definition television system and fifth generation computer project are now embarrassing classic cases of misguided government industrial policy. However, it is still true that in Japan the state's role in the economy is shared with the private sector, and both the public and private sectors have perfected means to make the market work for developmental goals.

Chapter 2

Knowledge Creation
Through Strategic Networks

Knowledge and the ability to continuously create knowledge are increasingly becoming two of the most important factors influencing competition. The already enormous accumulation of commercially usable knowledge worldwide will rapidly increase in the future. Drucker (1954, 1993) sees knowledge as significant not only because it represents one of several traditional production mediums—such as labor, capital, and land—but because it represents the only true resource. Badaracco (1991) inclines toward the same opinion, convinced that companies can and should have continuous access to the most diverse knowledge potentials to create and sustain long-term competitive advantages over other market participants. Similarly Nonaka and Takeuchi (1995) support the hypothesis that companies must be managed so that their co-workers exchange knowledge and thus create new ideas. Prerequisites for the creation of knowledge are the declared willingness of all participants to tolerate chaos, redundancy, and variety.

The classical pattern of strategic management is obviously no longer sufficient in view of the current distribution of knowledge. With increasing speed, knowledge is breaking firm boundaries, and practically every company has access to existing knowledge. The ability for creation and goal-oriented utilization of knowledge has become a primary challenge. According to Teramoto (1990), permeable organizations offer a good medium for creating and using knowledge. They activate the exchange of knowledge among the members of the organization and interact with other market participants in intercompany cooperatives. With this action they learn new models for rationalization. Permeable organizations perceive the plurality of knowledge more easily and react more sensitively to the changes in an organizational context.

This view of knowledge and the management of knowledge is based on Popper's critical rationalism which states that all knowledge is first assumed knowledge and all theories are hypotheses. Popper supports the view that knowledge and theories are valid only until they can be disproved through new discoveries and experiments (Popper, 1963). This means that the results of human actions do not have to be linked to original intentions. Popper (1945) supports organizations that promote solutions to problems because he believes existentialism is foremost a problem-solving process. He advocates organizational forms that allow different proposals to be distributed without restriction, then criticized and creatively changed.

In times of quick and far-reaching changes, organizational forms that support or stimulate the ability for progress and evolution of companies are in particular demand. Conventional, bureaucratically led companies are designed to suppress conflicts, to withstand changes, to negate, overlook, or trivialize problems. When problems are formulated, often a simple localization can be found (the colleagues, the neighboring department, the suppliers, the customers, the cooperation partners in the network). A system of defense that is based on scapegoating and nondiscussion is, by nature, a totalitarian system and thus mostly unsuitable for companies that are linked to their environment through cooperative agreements.

Teramoto (1990) indicates that a company whose strategy includes the goal of active integration into strategic networks can be more efficient than conventional competition strategies. Furthermore, he argues that the management of strategic networks requires openness and an ability to change because the business world is far less easily controlled and steered than a closed off, inwardly focused organization. Through the development of strategic networks, new and strong relationships are established between the organization and environment. The strict separation dissolves between the market and the hierarchy as opposite principles of the organization of collective and economic actions. The internal organization as the building block of linked organizations is built on the idea that change is absolutely possible. Structures are loosely linked and a decentralization and dehierarchization is constantly taking place. The differentiation into departments is being dissolved. The new organizational structures, if they can even still be categorized, demand an intensification of an informal, non-formalized communication. Project groups, partial autonomic production groups, and their networks secure both the production process as well as the innovation process.

The phenomenon of knowledge creation in strategic networks is viewed from three perspectives. The first perspective is *network culture*. According to Popper (1945) democratic businesses operate with a corporate culture allowing and promoting cooperative agreements in a network integration. Openness toward the inside and outside reduces the control mechanisms that are inherent with bureaucratic organizations. In these, it is expected that every action can be presented as a decision. This leads in part to exaggerated protection strategies and to conventional decisions. Bureaucratic organizations keep to themselves and do without cooperative agreements rather than share control and safety with other companies. They can rarely be regarded as a place in which decisions are made rationally.

The second perspective is that of *organizational learning*. Organizations are goal oriented. Perceived discrepancies between expected and factual values trigger discrepancies that lead to learning processes. With Popper's (1963) view that knowledge is presumably knowledge in need of continuous disapproval, organizations are caught in a vicious cycle of learning. The perception of the inadequacy of our own knowledge and the consequential striving for new knowledge is a learning process in itself. The goal of organizational evolution is to work toward better solutions which, when found, must always remain open for revision. In cooperative agreements, discrepancies can exist between the potential knowledge of the companies so that organizational learning inevitably sets in. It is, however, a prerequisite that the companies open up toward their environment and confront/accept the multilateral exchange of knowledge.

Cooperative competition is the third perspective being presented to the management of strategic networks in the sense of a purposely critical rationalism. This is a position between strict altruism and antagonistic Darwinism. Altruistic behavior would be an unanswered sacrifice of competitiveness to the benefit of the cooperating partners. Darwinism would be linked to egotistical behavior that is disrespectful of the abilities, requirements, and wishes of other market participants. Viewed from Popper's (1963) standpoint on critical rationalism, cooperative competition corresponds to the government form of democracy that simultaneously grants security and freedom. Competition is endangered by the totalitarian tendency of Darwinism, which Popper suspects in the government designs of the "wrong" prophets—Platon, Hegel, and Marx.

NETWORK CULTURE

Companies that have operated for years with the same established mechanisms of knowledge creation are increasingly finding themselves being pushed either into market niches or even totally out of the market. Many years of success often led to companies' no longer critically questioning the culturally founded behavior of economic actions. This approach was based on the conviction that all economic variables were predictable (Reich, 1991) and would remain constant (Sakaiya, 1991). The potential variety of knowledge was mostly negated.

The culture of a company as discussed in the newer literature about organizational theories (e.g., Mintzberg, 1989; Hamel and Prahalad, 1994; Nonaka and Takeuchi, 1995), apparently can be brought into close contact with the manner in which it generates knowledge. The development of corporate cultures is based on a virtually natural event. It is an increasingly central idea of companies' generating knowledge. In the corporate culture, the accumulation of similar experiences and decisions of individuals that make up a business are strengthened. This is not due to a dictatorship of mutual values, myths, and legends, but is the altered solution as Schein (1984) puts it, to the social construct of reality. Corporate cultures should be understood as models for basic assumptions that a company has developed in its efforts to deal with the problems of internal integration and adaptation to the external environment. Hofstede (1991) defines culture in this sense as collective programming of the brain that distinguishes between the members of different categories of people.

Nonaka and Takeuchi (1995) speak of a "culturally overlapping socialization," thus adding an outside perspective to the corporate culture as it is understood in the classical sense of a closed-off unit of the intracompany behavioral model. By this they mean that the point of reference of cultural behavior spreads to the surroundings of the business, especially to the cooperative partners. If companies within a strategic network want to create knowledge mutually, they must "speak the same language," which means they have to follow similar cultural behavioral models. It is not surprising that cultural friction (Pucik, 1988; Jones and Shill, 1991; Parkhe, 1992) can be found especially among international alliances between companies that belong to different cultural circles or markets. These can often lead to failure in the management of cooperative relationships.

If the idea of a culturally overlapping socialization is specific to strategic networks, an intertwined corporate culture or a "network culture" sets in. The cooperating companies share certain models and goals of cultural actions. The expansion of the concept of the corporate culture to that of the network culture is based on the view that an organization does not *have* a culture but rather *is* a culture (Smircich, 1983). Corporate culture is usually regarded as a shaping parameter of the real, sociotechnical system and thus it is established that an organization or a business has a culture. The idea that an organization is a culture does not include the corporate culture as a variable but as a new, basic concept leading to realization. To understand the behavior of culture as a social goal- and task-oriented system, the internal links of the system and its interactions with the environment must be recognized.

The interactions between companies in strategic networks constitute a mutual culture, experienced by all involved companies. A strict economic view (an organization *has* a culture) blocks the access to the social context of companies that, according to Drucker (1993), is necessary to build the trust and commitment needed for maintaining cooperations. In a theory of markets and organizations, learning and trust may well take the place that efficiency and opportunism occupy in the theory of markets and hierarchies, while purpose may take the place of price.

The *network culture* is structured into three parts. In *cultural opening and variety* the concept of a network culture is defined. In *interactions between companies* the mechanism which serves as the model for working together between companies is identified. Finally, in *cultural emancipation* the dissolution of companies from the cultural stigmatism of bureaucratic organizations is described. A network culture can neither be made nor purposely manipulated since only cooperation in strategic networks leads to mutually experienced cultural models of behavior. Companies, however, can change the organizational context conditions to smooth the way to a new cultural understanding by opening up to their environment through the commitment to a cooperative relationship.

Cultural Opening and Variety

Over time, companies work out an action-directed culture (Schein, 1984). This culture defines company internal norms and values and influences the resources and strategies necessary for its achievement. The culture of a company includes values and norms for the regulation of social behavior. The observation and anchoring of the values and norms usually occurs via symbols.

Symbols are signs that portray a certain meaningful content and that in addition to a purely denotative context can also portray more complex communication ideas. In their book, *Corporate Culture and Organizational Symbolism*, Alevsson and Berg (1992) show that symbols portray the values of human societies that try to utilize them to distinguish themselves from others in their environment. Cultural artifacts (e.g., art) as human actions (e.g., language, rituals) are the perfect carriers for symbols. In this way symbols communicate the context that makes sense (connection of meaning) of human experience.

Cultural symbols can be mediated beyond the edge of an organization. The perspective of a network culture relies on the opening of a company into the cultural variety of a network association. While the concept of a corporate culture is limited to a single business, the network culture manifests itself as a cultural bracket around those businesses that cooperate in a network. Figure 2.1 clarifies the cultural opening of a business through integration into a strategic network.

FIGURE 2.1. Cultural Opening

corporate culture

network culture

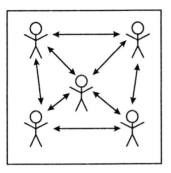

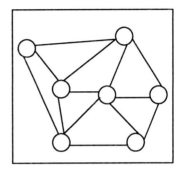

intraorganizational
linking

interorganizational
linking

The variety of corporate cultures that coexist and interact in a network is represented by different organizational lifestyles in which individual philosophies and perceptions are expressed. Thus a communication and understanding problem arises through this cultural meeting in which acceptance and trust become the first necessary steps to its alleviation. The multicultural dialog is not so much a problem solution as a requirement for the possibility of understanding other companies and thus reflect its own culture through the perception of others. A better understanding of one's own corporate culture enables the development of multicultural dialogue processes in a network culture made up of a number of companies. The same is true in reverse. The single corporate culture must at least have the complexity of the surrounding network culture.

Here the importance of the concept of "requisite variety" comes into play. The law of requisite variety states that the variety of a system must be at least equally as large as the variety of the environment to which it is trying to adjust (Maruyama, 1992). Similarly, Ashby (1958) holds the opinion that variety can only be regulated by variety. The necessary variety is the reason that organizations strive to maintain a sufficient amount of diversity in order to properly grasp the variety that surrounds them. They must be flexible enough to make use of the variety found in the business vicinity and integrate it as requisite variety.

Strategic networks are not products of their environment but rather products of the cultural self-production of the company members. A network is mainly focused on itself, thereby determining its position in the economic field and protecting itself from the culturally different environment. Thus, the formation of networks is not determined from the outside but merely pushed in a certain direction. Further development is dependent on the cultural analysis of the companies bound into the network. During this analysis a mutual culture is generated—a network culture—that cannot be easily understood by outsiders. The network culture stabilizes the network on the inside through escape barriers and lends autonomy and boundaries on the outside through entrance barriers. A mutual language lends cultural identity and works as a barrier against intrusion and escape.

The companies of the Mitsui-*keiretsu* are good examples of how a network culture is created and operated. Single companies work along similar internal guidelines and rules. One of the guidelines, the principle of legality, has a binding effect for all company members. Further signs of a binding network culture visible to the outside are identical abbreviations for departments and positions, similar organizational structures and management principles, and an anchoring of inner company behavior samples in the corporate culture of the Kansai region. Mitsui, one of Japan's oldest *keiretsu*, has always valued the cultural identity of the Kansai area (area around Osaka, Kobe, and Kyoto) to distance itself from the companies of the Mitsubishi-*keiretsu* that are headquartered in Tokyo. It is important that the cultural behavioral models of the Mitsui-*keiretsu* first formed historically and thus are the product of the dialogue between the single companies.

According to Mintzberg (1989), organizations need established communication processes for predictable events to even become an organization. Without structure, there is no membership and without membership, no organization. Organizations need to clearly define members to be able to develop structure.

Often it is extremely difficult to draw the line between membership and nonmembership. As Davis and Meyer (1997) state, it is a problem of the blurring of lines between companies and network and between network and environment. It is about the fact that knowledge-generating companies only have thin, penetrable, and porous barriers against the outside world (Drucker, 1993). The reception of market mechanisms into the internal organizational processes and the evacuation of internal processes make it increasingly difficult to distinguish between organization and environment. The mechanisms of intra- and interorganizational interactions and coordination overlap one another. The constant threat of self-elimination becomes concrete in all parts of the company in which processes of generation of knowledge took place. This becomes apparent in such central areas as the relationship to other companies, the territorial definition of the network, and the definition of the network membership.

Although the determination of membership and nonmembership in a strategic network through formal and less formal agreements is a basic prerequisite for the existence of a network organization, it is not sufficient to provide vitality. A network organization, like any other organization, is created through its interactions (Hakansson, 1989; Gilroy, 1993). Interactions are its elixir of life. Through these, various opportunities become reality. For a network organization to differentiate itself from loose and accidental connections, interactions must be oriented along certain cultural norms and identities. Through the linkage of organizational boundaries, decisions, norms, and identities, strategic networks obtain a greater stability as opposed to spontaneous interactions, since single companies can establish a mutual culture. Thus the network culture is an expression of a continuing interaction of the companies bound into the network and is at the same time the result of past interactions and requisite for future interactions. The interactions act to preserve the cultural identity of the strategic network and to confirm the interactions already made.

Thus, the network culture can be seen as the stabilizing element of strategic networks. Interactions between companies always affect past interactions and are simultaneously bound to the cultural history of the network. Networks exist in their cultural latency; they are updated through concrete situations, present their conclusions willingly and openly, and then dissolve again.

Interfirm Interactions

Western firms, viewed from a black-and-white general perspective, rarely have problems in changing their business partners from one moment to the next as soon as such a change yields advantages. Based on this attitude, no arrangement for the mutual relationship other than the contracted one can be considered since the number of possible partners to choose from can be almost any size.

It would be foolish to enter a relationship based on loyalty and faith; loyalty and faith can only exist between partners that are linked together indefinitely, know each other exactly, and are dependent upon one another through mutual interests. As shown by the studies of Teramoto (1990), Miyashita and Russel (1994), Sai (1995), and Scher (1997), partnerships in Japan last longer than partnerships in Western countries. Western partnerships place more emphasis on the objective quality of price and product in economic transactions than on the partners of the transactions.

Relationships between companies can be interpreted as economic business transactions. According to the traditional view of a perfect competitors' society, business transactions are carried out in an autonomous market (Gemünden, Ritter, and Walter, 1998). In agreement with newer organizational research, however, purchasing transactions can be understood as interactive exchange (Johanson and Mattson, 1987; Hakansson, 1989). Cooperative partners are connected by stable relationships marked by medium- and long-range goals. The adaptation capabilities of the participating companies in the interaction process and the social component of the relationship are of extreme importance for the success of a cooperative. Zahra, Garvis, and George (1999) define the way in which a company develops its relationships with others as "social capital."

Cooperative relationships in strategic networks are usually not simple stimulus-response relationships, but rather are contracted for the long term. These relationships develop certain patterns of efficiency that become established over time. The linked companies feel affiliated with a cooperative relationship. The use of language (e.g., "we are expanding our relationship to company X") and rituals (e.g., celebrating the ten-year existence of a relationship) indicate that cooperative relationships usually fulfill the criteria for loyalty and mutual obligation. Cooperative relationships can thus be seen as the result of interaction processes between members of cooperating companies. Past interactions act to cement future interactions. Loyalty can thus be seen as a purposeful behavior to postpone the termination of a cooperative relationship since an emotional tie to the partner exists. The partners show commitment toward a mutual goal.

Companies can stabilize relationships in a network by trying to further bind the partners to them. The strategy of binding a partner is an attempt to limit the decisional possibilities of that partner for the sake of the bilateral cooperative. This can be done by increasing the "cost for leaving" of the partner, or at least by pointing it out. Japanese automobile manufacturers always refer to the protective integration of the Toyota or Nissan "family" and demonstrate the advantages of such a dependent relationship. Of course by doing so, they imply that in the event of a dissolution of the exclusive partnership, the supplying companies are left "unprotected" and "without a master." There is a term in Japan for this concept, the so-called *ronin*. They are persons or organizations that have lost their social ties. The concept is derived from the forty-seven *ronin*, a legend from ancient Edo, today's Tokyo.

> A knight was involuntarily caught in intrigues at the court of the Shogun and stood in front of the state dignitaries as a man who had lost face. He only had one possibility to restore his honor, that of committing ritual suicide, which was not uncommon in ancient Japan. The Shogun thus confiscated his worldly goods, and his vassals were from now on considered knights without a master, *ronin*. The *ronin* later avenged their master, but also committed suicide since they had lost their social link. The forty-seven *ronin* are a microscopic reflection of the social network and mutual dependency in Japanese society. Even in modern Japan, loyalty as the measure to prove oneself still is held in high esteem.

A wide spectrum of possibilities exists in binding a cooperative partner, from the exclusive binding with contracts to the purpose binding. With the latter, the company purposely accepts restrictions because the service in return is attractive enough to compensate the loss of autonomy. The characteristic "attraction," also includes low risk, which might appear to the outsider as inflexibility. The exclusive binding is often a relationship that excludes voluntary follow-up actions from the start or at least makes them very unlikely. The purpose binding can be built upon, as the company emphasizes past performances, appeals to the moral values of the partner, and thus searches for a voluntary binding of the partner.

The actions of all companies in the network are interwoven with one another beyond bilateral ties. For example, if a firm of the Toyota production network removes itself from the latent dependency by building up a supplier relationship with Nissan, this will also have consequences for the other suppliers. The suppliers could see the advantages of such an action and could use it as an example. A strategic network generates complex relationships among the companies. As single-action takers they have no independent influence on the network. Only the totality of company-to-company interactions determines the behavior, characteristics, and condition of the network. This is why the action potential of a network, as Hakansson (1989) points out, is not equivalent to the sum of the actions of single companies. Rather, the crosswise interwoven interactions are fundamental for the existence of higher-action models. The Mitsubishi-*keiretsu*, for example, is characterized by a strong homogeneity of strategic decision processes of the firm's member. Often a violation of the mutual action codex is responded to with a reference to the mutual network culture.

The interaction of two companies in a strategic network cooperative is portrayed in Figure 2.2. The firms interact in such a way that they only trigger interactions that do not endanger their own exis-

FIGURE 2.2. Interfirm Interaction in Strategic Networks

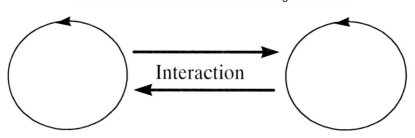

tence. Thus they interchangeably become the origin of interactions. The individual development of the firms is linked and the interactions mesh with one another. As shown in the writings of Hakansson and Snehota (1995), relationships among cooperative partners can be developed with the goal of increasing economic output and efficiency of the entire network. As the relationships become more intensive and thus longer lasting over time in terms of quality and quantity, they develop into a stable, mutual, socially dependent relationship. First, the deepening of a relationship extends toward other latently existing relationships. Second, results of actions can be directly attributed to a relationship. Examples from everyday language include: a relationship "expands," "is going well or bad," "is breaking up," etc. Third, one is concerned about the follow-up possibilities of actions; this means the relationship has a future. Interactions between companies are indeed, as Mattsson (1987) puts it, the basis for stability and change in strategic networks.

Cultural Emancipation

The ideas of culture as an independent part of economic actions and economic actions as a segment of culture are slowly gaining suitable importance in the scientific arena of economic theory. An example may be found in the contingency theory of Lawrence and Lorsch (1967) and in the transaction cost theory of Williamson (1975) that theory and company practice are culturally invariant. The interpretation of the term culture and the role of culture as an independent variable that explains the different shaping of management functions in different cultures with linking hypotheses is further disputed.

Hofstede's studies (Hofstede, 1980; 1991) regarding questions of the character of culture and its action and methodology of cultural analysis in an organizational context have led to a change. This change has removed the term corporate culture from the confined area of a single company that operates within the market of the same country. In the meantime, different aspects of organizational theory give rise to questions that originally were only raised within cultural scientific discussions. Redding (1994), for example, assumes that empirical occurrences are mostly understandable within the framework of their cultural environment, and thus are rarely comparable beyond the boundaries of a country. Every culture has developed its own system of values and norms that is equal to other systems. Something that is considered a typical behavioral form in one culture can be seen as abnormal by a member of another culture. Corporate cultures should be seen as a subsystem of the national culture of a country, whereby boundary-spanning activities wipe out the determinants of a corporate culture as the reflection of a country culture.

Czarniawska-Joerges (1992) states that companies are organizations that, comparable to living organisms, can display specific evolutionary potentials. During the course of a company's evolution, different states of cultural behavioral systems develop and are practiced so that the cultural identity of a company can present itself very differently. Organizations are also cultures and the evolution of organizations is closely related to the specific change of these cultures.

Similarly, Alevsson and Berg (1992) support the thesis that the cultural evolution of organizations includes phases of development as well as phases of stagnation. Stagnation can result from the lack of willingness to change because of a relatively stable market situation or a dominant market position. Experiences that a company has accumulated through successful and unsuccessful solutions to problems are transferred to the present in the form of unwritten laws.

One possible way to fight cultural stagnation is to enter into cooperative agreements in a strategic network. Figure 2.3 clarifies this connection.

Companies that are self-contained and operate along conventional avenues of strategic management often find themselves in a position of relative stagnation and paralysis since they possess relatively stable corporate cultures. Repetition and stability are, according to Weick (1987), structural limitations of one's decisional connections. This phenomenon is strongest when a single piece of information is sufficient to know the entire organization and to predict its behavior. The organization is geared toward safety, to the creation of certainty, and to the minimizing of risks. New employees bring unwelcome restlessness; familiar suppliers and customers are preferred, and cooperation between companies is seen as a potential source of destabilization. Companies that favor security and stability have a histo-

FIGURE 2.3. Cultural Emancipation Through Strategic Networks

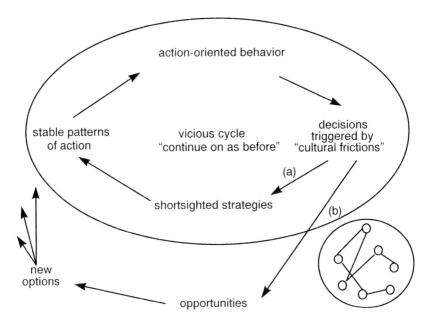

Key: (a) option to stay within the circle
     (b) option for emancipation

ry of trying to preserve culture. They distance themselves from the anarchy of total freedom by diminishing the span of opportunities and decreasing the number of solutions that could evolve.

Mintzberg (1989) has reconstructed an example of a typical management day. The employees of a company usually work at relentless speed; their actions are marked by short-lived, ever-changing circumstances and interruptions, and they are very action oriented. In short, they do not reflect the cultural model of their actions. "Foreign" cultures are not even admitted into the organization. Strategic decisions are often made out of the necessity of removing cultural friction, and mistakes are made in the pursuit of a smooth course to the extent that a company becomes internalized in every aspect. These strategies are mostly of a short-lived nature since the corporate culture itself must not be questioned.

Such a vicious cycle seems to be a good description of the cultural daily life in a company. Action oriented, feeble, and fragmented, relative confusion is accompanied by an inclination to reflect what will draw attention. Cultural friction—caused by "culturally different people" within the company or outside of it—draws attention. This is where its function lies. If it is accompanied by short-term and highly limited solution strategies, it is used and sought too little in its functionality. Obviously this vicious cycle is rarely useful in processing complex problems. The traditional answer at this point is the establishment of report, analytical, and solution systems and to search for stable solutions that can strengthen the corporate culture. However, all endeavors are undermined if cultural friction still has a good chance to become the dominating priority.

As a solution, the purposeful instigation of cultural friction presents itself by entering cooperative agreements into strategic networks. Differences in the cultural behavior of the cooperative partners can be used to ascertain the actual roots of the problems. By going from an egocentric corporate culture to a latently open and reflective network culture, the potential for the generation of continuing knowledge suddenly improves dramatically. The instigation of cultural friction should not be mistaken for a provocation of possible competitors, but is meant as a communicative that unfolds differences relevant to problem solving. Without ignoring differences and logic, the company must unfold, produce, and make use of Popper's (1963) question: What can lead to a better solution of the problems?

Viewing cultural friction as a cause and as input, new options to create the daily routines appear. Employees find themselves in cooperative agreements that are the source of differing views and routines. It is not simply enough to fall back on old cultural behavioral models such as "this is how it has always been done." If such an attitude takes over, the cooperative is destined to fail. Entering cooperative agreements within strategic networks can lead to cultural emancipation and a culture of constant change.

With the possibility of cultural emancipation, a network culture can be defined as the sophisticated solution of interactions among companies in a strategic network and its cultural transformation. Only continuous interaction enables the development of a mutually perceivable cultural identity of the cooperative partners. The mutual identity is not determined by a central authority but develops through equalization of different norms, courses, and structures. Individual companies open themselves to a critical examination through the partner companies. In this sense, network cultures are essentially pluralistic.

Which mechanism guarantees the continuation of interactions remains an open question. How can companies accumulate new knowledge that can catapult their company's culture out of stagnation? In the next chapter we will try to answer that question.

ORGANIZATIONAL LEARNING

One of Popper's (1963) central theories is that problem solving and falsification are acts of learning. He assumes that making mistakes is indeed human and that mistakes are almost certainly provoked through falsification. Any historical examples of human failure are examples of the progression of knowledge. In this sense, any discovery of a mistake is a real advance in knowledge. One can learn from mistakes; criticism is the only way to discover mistakes and to learn from them. Popper appears to have discovered that learning is a turning point to something different, not necessarily to something better. The process of learning is influenced by a broad constellation of social, political, and structural variables, so that the apparent truth, implicated by newfound knowledge, can become the victim of critical examination.

It is obvious that dogmatic organizations and their bureaucratic structures see the process of learning as a hinderance, since existing products, action models, and cultural values are regarded as the only truth and are defended against criticism. The hindering of learning behavior is a restriction to routines formed by dogmatism. Decisions are formed by being compatible with the routines rather than through the search for new, innovative action models. The concept of dogmatism is based on the idea that truth is to be made equal to facts that coincide with the truth. It is clear that such a concept can only be supported by absolute, objective truths and thus by a stable world image. In an organization entangled in dogmatism there is no room for learning processes. Following norms is strictly enforced and vacillating behavior, which could be used to gain new experiences is not tolerated. In an extreme case, the organizations become so stiff and incapable of change that they break apart when the pressure becomes too great.

Companies integrated into a network more often leave the search for knowledge to the internal organizational units and the other network participants. Competition forces companies to continually adjust to the changing circumstances by further developing existing knowledge within the companies and by pulling potentially useful knowledge from the cooperative agreements and upgrading it. Learning in strategic networks in itself is a paradox: the quick spreading of knowledge within the network leads to the fact that the "learned" competitive headstart of a company is always ruined again. This knowledge leads to the fact that the wheel of the acquisition of knowledge must always turn faster for the company to remain competitive. Probably the only lasting advantage of competition can be seen in one company learning more quickly than another.

In the cognitive theories of human learning (compare, e.g., Piaget, 1978) it can be shown that knowledge and understanding not only grow from registering observations, but that simultaneously lasting restructuring in the individuals involved in the process takes place. The cognitive structures are being reflected in the conscious actions of humans, since learned values and action principles exist behind every action.

This insight, which developed for individual actions, was transferred to the organizational theory by Argyris and Schön (1978) and Hedberg (1981). Members of one organization communicate among themselves and thereby change their own behavior and that of the entire organization. This is also referred to as *organizational learning*. Just like individuals, companies must continuously face new aspects of their environment and react to them proactively by unlearning old practiced behavioral models and acquiring new models. Organizational learning is, as Senge (1990) states, the necessary mechanism to secure the survival of companies in the long run.

Individual Identity and Organization

The employees of large Japanese firms usually do not work in the same company department during their entire career as do employees of Western companies (Pucik, 1988; Reading, 1992). In comparison, they often switch departments and are usually, if possible, moved through many job areas of the company. An employee from the R&D department also learns new tasks in the marketing department to understand how the products developed by him or her are marketed. Such changes in working areas take place in periodical intervals, so that the employees constantly have to acquire new abilities. This procedure benefits the flow of information in the company, since knowledge can be transferred from one department to the next. The organization itself, and not only the individual employees, is integrated into learning processes. As the literature confirms, Japanese companies seem to utilize the processes of organizational learning consciously and deliberately (Nonaka and Johansson, 1985; Kagono et al., 1985; Teramoto, 1990; Nonaka and Takeuchi, 1995; Fruin, 1997).

In forming and optimizing their business processes, companies require a broad spectrum of knowledge, which they use for the fulfillment of tasks and problem solving. According to Walsh and Ungson (1991), the collective memory of companies plays an important role in the utilization of learning processes. Every current experience is based on the past knowledge of previous experiences. Current experiences are thus always interpreted with a certain past understanding in mind. Cognitive orientations that can be interpreted as routine are rooted in the collective memory of a company. Analogous to the individual cognitive structure, these routines steer and organize the perception of signals through the organization. Organizational routines outlast employee fluctuations and are handed down by written instructions, but are also passed on through the socialization of new employees. The frame of reference in which routines are lived thus has to be changed dramatically. In this sense, learning means perceiving the internal organization as well as the environment differently.

Despite all efforts to establish a general theory of organizational learning, this field of science is still in its early stages. A widely accepted and sound starting point is that of Argyris and Schön (1978), which serves as the basis for further arguments. According to Argyris and Schön, organizational learning happens through a change in the organizational knowledge saved in the collective memory. The expectations of the participants of the organization toward the consequences of their actions are established in action routines (theory in use). During their perception they check their expectations with their construction of reality and "learn or un-learn" them by constructing, testing, and reconstructing their mental models according to their action routines. The approach hereby assumes different learning orders in which the construction of reality can take place (see Figure 2.4).

Learning of the first order involves all processes that create a potential for adaptation. Through a feedback process, the organizational members act adaptively within the limits of their action routines. The learning processes go through tracks of preformed models without changing these, however. Based on the routines, experienced differences between expectations and reality are gradually minimized. First order learning then happens within the psychological system of the individuals without changing their interaction model within the organization. Measurable criteria for the success of such learning processes then is the internal efficiency.

Second order learning can lead an organization to create new and innovative models of action. The process of correction between expectations and reality happens discursively among the organizational members and leads to an institutionalization of changed mod-

FIGURE 2.4. Learning Orders

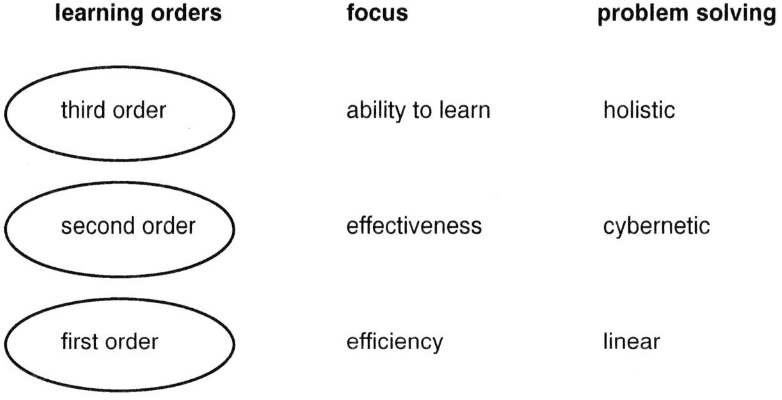

learning orders	focus	problem solving
third order	ability to learn	holistic
second order	effectiveness	cybernetic
first order	efficiency	linear

els of action. Essentially, new ground will be walked on due to the change of values and routines which will open up an appropriate frame of action and will thus increase the effectiveness of the organization as a whole. Second order learning is characterized cybernetically, since the adaptation of reality to wishful goals is continuously undertaken.

Finally, the third order of learning is made up of the identification and development of learning processes. Learning of the third order is part of a holistic problem solution idea, "meta-learning," or a "learning to learn," since both previous learning processes themselves become objects of contemplation. Symbolic events are re-read, concepts reinterpreted, and the points of reference for learning occurrences changed. With third order learning the ability of an organization to learn is improved. The question not only arises whether an organization learns, but whether it is learning fast enough to fulfill its use. This can happen especially through removing learning barriers and stimulating the willingness to learn.

Only in rare cases will third order learning directly lead to a "cultural revolution." It is more likely to be a stepwise development until a balance between wanted and actual behavior has occurred. The amount and the necessary speed of third order learning especially depend on the gap between the established culture and its environment. The influence of the corporate culture on the learning processes is relatively undisputed (Keough and Doman, 1992). It influences the interpretation models used to process experiences with its norms, and determines the filtering of information. If, for example, the identification of a certain product or technology is an integral part of the corporate culture, signals for changes are often not perceived for a long time. Only after the failure is unmistakable is one willing to make changes. This can, however, take a very long time. When meta-learning as learning of the third order sets in, it can already be too late for the company. By the time the newly learned mechanisms have been translated into products, the market can already have turned in a different direction. This is very different in companies whose basic conviction is that only change in itself can be lasting. In these companies changes in all three learning orders are being taken up with no reservations.

Argyris and Schön also call the three orders of learning single-loop, double-loop, and deutero learning. A multitude of typologies might differ by name, but barely by content. For the further development of a starting point of organizational learning in strategic networks, it shall, for clarity reasons, be referred to as learning of first, second, and third order.

It should be kept in mind that organizations learn in such a way as to differ from the sum of all individual learning processes (Hedberg, 1981). Just because organizational members individually learn and continually increase their knowledge does not mean that the behavior of the organization as such is undergoing change as well. Important for the transition of individual to organizational learning is the collective perception of a goal that works to stimulate the co-workers. Individual learning processes are necessary but not sufficient to make organizational learning possible.

Organizational knowledge merely includes the knowledge that is actually at the disposal of the company for the solution of tasks and problems. Helleloid and Simonin (1994) conclude from this that an enlargement of the knowledge base can occur if existing intra-organizational knowledge can be activated, or extra-organizational knowledge as is latently found in cooperative partners can be pulled into the organization and thus be utilized. In this sense vertical learning processes, which are carried out within the boundaries of a company, must be distinguished from horizontal learning processes as carried out in a network structure. Organizational learning thus describes the enlargement of an integrated, communicable, and consensual base of knowledge.

Vertical Learning Processes

Companies in further discussions should be understood as organizations made up of three knowledge levels: innovations, competencies, and cultures. This division is based on an abstraction of possible goal systems that can exist context dependent in an organization.

Competencies and cultures are based on the operative goal to bring out innovations. According to Hippel (1988) and Mintzberg (1989), innovations should be understood as concrete products and processes that bring out reform targeted to an increase in one's competitive ability. Such an understanding about the nature of innovations is not new. Schumpeter (1934) has discussed the innovative combination of new goods, production methods, markets, supplier sources, and organizational forms. Innovations are directly targeted at an increase in the ability to compete, while having a direct guiding function for the company's achievement construct.

In the resource-based approach to strategy by Hamel and Prahalad (1994), competencies play a central role as a further organizational element. They see central competencies as the growth medium for the progress of innovations. Central competencies can be understood as accumulations of abilities to react to new market demands quickly and efficiently and to use an accumulated and responsive knowledge base for the creation of new products and businesses. Although they do not diminish with use, they must be well kept, cared for, and also used since they can be unlearned otherwise. Central competencies are broader than innovations. They are the basis for product developments that at first seem unprognostical. They allow entrance to different markets, substantially add to the usage value of innovations, and can only be copied with great difficulty. They are less based on the present than are innovations, represent a future potential, and thus are perceived as strategic triumphs in a continuing competitive field.

Competencies are based on a culture as a normal scale in which values attached to a company are explained. This culture is simultaneously the foundation on which competencies can develop. Through vertical learning processes, innovations can be derived from competencies and organizational cultures changed, which in turn stimulate the formation of competencies. The flow of knowledge is thus a cybernetic process that is more characterized by feedback based on learning processes than by goals set voluntarily.

The levels of knowledge are sequentially lined up against one another and connected by learning processes. One must distinguish between deductive, generative, and evolutionary learning. These learning processes can be interpreted as stabilizing connecting parts between cultures, competencies, and innovations. The experiences won through innovative processes and the development of competencies have an effect on the corporate culture and thus on the organization in its entirety. In the context of vertical learning processes, the possible learning orders present the picture seen in Figure 2.5.

Companies create product and process innovations from their competencies through deductive learning. According to the procedure of deduction, special knowledge is derived from general knowledge. Deductive learning is a first order learning process since knowledge is extracted from already existing knowledge, from competencies, and product and process innovations. The expertise connected to competencies is integrated into concrete products and processes. Since this expertise is spread among many co-workers, organizational learning does not remain the job of a few, but rather is realized by the organization that continues to learn

FIGURE 2.5. Vertical Learning Processes

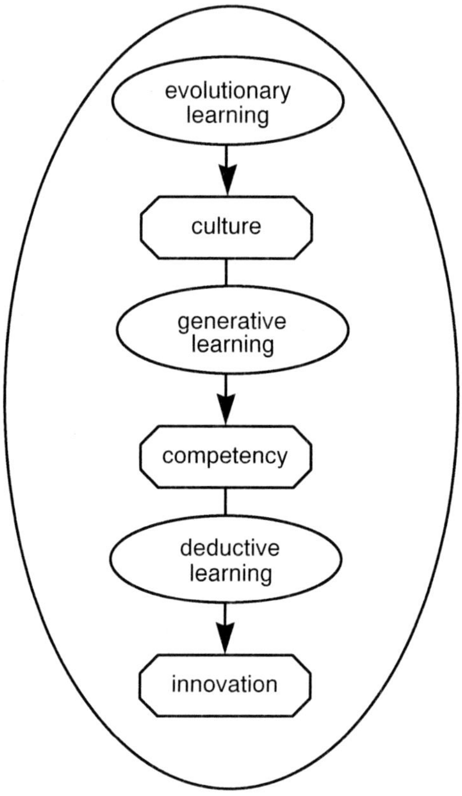

in its entirety (Senge, 1990). With the idea of deductive learning, customer wishes can be responded to quickly since competencies have the potential for necessary specifications. Technologies can be mastered by integrating them into existing competencies.

Generative learning is a second order learning process. This is primarily not about concrete useful innovations, but about the acquisition of competencies. The success of the company is based on diversification of competencies that can be spread over several business units. Experiences from different units are put together so that the further distribution of knowledge will be forced. The corporate culture functions as a higher and supporting level of knowledge that holds fundamental creativity potential for the generation of knowledge (Garvin, 1993). The members of the organization interact and exchange knowledge, which is compressed to a collective knowledge and worked into competencies. The strength and character of a corporate culture strongly correlates with the ability for generative learning. As the carrier of collective knowledge, the corporate culture can limit or support learning in many different ways.

If companies are not capable of successfully installing and caring for competencies, this can be due to their corporate culture, which only supports innovation and motivates its co-workers in a limited way. Since the ability to learn manifests itself just as much in a corporate culture, a new orientation of learning processes should advisably start with an analysis and perhaps a redefinition of the corporate culture (Weick, 1987). To secure their innovative power in the long run, the companies can realize a strengthening of their competencies through a paradigmatic change of the corporate culture. Thus evolutionary learning is the learning of new ways of life, and according to this logic, a third order learning. The members of the organization unlearn the guidelines and cognitive models of past learning processes and acquire new models.

Deductive, generative, and evolutionary learning occur within the organizational boundaries of a company whereby the single learning sequences can set in simultaneously as an "up and down" on a ladder of the different knowledge levels. The level of evolutionary learning facilitates the best possible use of knowledge potentials that are intertwined with cultural behavioral patterns. It is farthermost from the dominating deductive learning of daily life, which describes the translation into direct usable products and processes. Generative learning is on the middle level and symbolizes all processes that deal with the development of competencies.

The vertical learning process is not free of conflicts. Analyzing and doubting old success recipes, it functions as a filter of the corporate culture. Vertical learning also poses questions of which direction to learn or forget, which of the existing products and competencies still have future potential, and with which abilities they should be supplemented. This can lead to substantial power and interest conflicts. Starting too early can mean a quick end to the initiation of the learning process. To wait until necessity and direction are apparent to everyone can also lead the company into a deep crisis. Vertical learning processes cannot be prescribed since they require a broad involvement and discussion in the entire company.

Horizontal Learning Processes

Aside from vertical learning processes, companies have the potential to initiate horizontal learning processes. When companies find themselves together in a cooperative to undertake marketing, production, and/or product development together, they can learn the knowledge resources of the partner companies (Lorange and Roos, 1992). Since an important goal of a cooperative is the unification of complementary knowledge resources, the companies have an elementary interest in internalizing the knowledge resources of their partners. If companies can cleverly strengthen their knowledge pool through horizontal learning, they improve their chances of competitiveness. For the duration of a cooperative agreement, the organizational boundaries of the partner companies partially merge with one another, so that they are presented with an opportunity to acquire the inside knowledge of the partner. The success of commitment in strategic networks is thus also always dependent on the learning ability between companies.

As in vertical learning processes, there are also three orders of learning that have different degrees of complexity in the horizontal learning processes. First, adaptive learning describes the internalization of product and process innovations. In the second step, stimulative learning, the competencies of the companies are supplemented and further developed by cooperative activities, so that second order learning processes become active. The third learning sequence, interpretive learning, requires more than the pure transfer of existing knowledge modules. The culturally based behavior of the partner companies is questioned for transferability, their own corporate culture is further developed, and new perceptions in reference to the business are formed. During the process of cooperation, the company unlearns usual learning methods and acquires new models of learning. The three dimensions of horizontal learning are portrayed in Figure 2.6.

Adaptive learning is a first order learning mode, since learning essentially occurs as an imitation of the innovations of the partner companies. Usually cooperating companies define exactly which products and processes shall and may be internalized by the partner company and which ones may not. This is why in certain areas of production competition remains intact, while there is cooperation in others (Pucik, 1988; Hamel, 1991). Employees are sent into a cooperative with the goal to localize and learn the technologies of the partner that were brought into the cooperative agreement. In the event that one of the partners learns more quickly and effectively

FIGURE 2.6. Horizontal Learning Processes

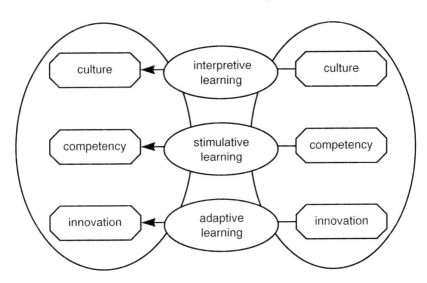

than the other, discrepancies can easily arise in a cooperative agreement. For this reason the co-workers should be sensitized for their special learning duties. Appearances of discrepancies between the partners can thus be kept to a minimum.

Cooperation between companies is not limited to the internalization of product and process innovations, but can expand to the acquisition of competencies. Cooperative partners cannot be selected according to their primary usefulness for the strengthening of the technologies of a business unit, but for the strengthening of competencies of the business as a whole. The partners with stimulative learning processes, as opposed to the cooperative agreements in which partners make do with the acquisition of product or process innovations, step into an extremely difficult, yet at the same time highly effective terrain, since cooperation between companies can influence the competitive ability in a lasting way. Such cooperative agreements are often time-restricted interest communities, which develop out of the understanding that antagonistic competition can be a disadvantage for the company (Teramoto, Richter, and Iwasaki, 1993). Common business understanding and intensive partnership, however, can strengthen the competencies of the cooperating companies in the long run. Stimulative learning is second order learning, since members of the organization react to impulses of the external environment with the development of collectively produced knowledge potentials.

In interpretive learning, the relationship between the actions of the organization and the resulting findings is changed because of the constant interpretation of the corporate culture of the cooperative partners. Thus learning turns into the object of learning. The learning models of the partner companies are critically checked and, if need be, internalized to improve their own abilities for vertical learning processes. Daft and Huber (1987) believe that knowledge which is outside of the organizational boundaries of a company has no meaning as long as it is not internalized and interpreted by the company. In this sense, organizations are not mere systems of data transmission, but rather systems that give data a meaning. The corporate culture provides all necessary interpretation modules to learn the culturally based behavioral models of the cooperative partners. Interpretative learning finally can lead to a paradigmatic change of the corporate culture.

Adaptive, simulative, and interpretive learning starts at the organizational boundaries of companies, which means at the transition of individual companies to the domain of strategic networks. Companies act in a complex environment of knowledge in which no company can exist anymore without an awareness of the knowledge potential of the others. To compete means to position one's own company in a strategic network rather than to penetrate markets with aggressive strategies. The generation of knowledge through horizontal learning processes occurs in an area between cooperation and competition: cooperative competition.

COOPERATIVE COMPETITION

Darwinism as an evolutionary survival strategy is no scientifically proven theory for Popper (1945; 1963), but rather a metaphysical research program. A Darwinistic concept, according to which living beings have to react with antagonistic behavior in order to survive, contradicts Popper's idea that living beings produce solutions to problems themselves. The solutions to problems do not necessarily have to lead to competition. Many examples in nature prove that certain species refrain from antagonistic behavior as long as other creatures in their environment do the same. Furthermore, symbiotic life forms exist that are based on the principle of mutual utilization of critical resources. Problem solutions, however, are always subject to selection pressure; this means they are only useful until their insufficiency has been proven.

Popper is against a direct transfer of Darwinism into social systems, since social evolution does not start with the individual but with rules and practices. On a social level, human conscience and language play a role as new categories. People do not personally disappear with their mistakes, but can let formulated hypotheses "die" by critically questioning, and if necessary, falsifying them. Social evolution develops along a line between falsification and verification or is projected into survival strategies based on social evolution. It is a balance between competition and cooperation. Depending on an individual's environmental situation, the pendulum can swing stronger toward competition or cooperation when reasons for the verification of a directional change arise. Thus, the basic strategy of human actions is cooperative competition. Verification and falsification move in correspondence with a gradual evolution, because according to Popper (1963), any planning is piecework in a vacuum of cooperation and competition.

Similar to individual actions, the dispute between cooperation and competition among companies is an economic reality. One will rarely find a pursuit of one of these strategies without compromises. The integration into a strategic network transfers companies into a balance of cooperative competition. Often cooperation takes place only in partial areas, such as in a certain product group or in defined market segments, while competition remains intact in others.

Cooperation was traditionally seen only as the second-best solution to increase competitive ability. Dissociation strategies were preferred to cooperative strategies for a long time. At the end of the 1980s, however, an avalanche of cooperative agreements set in so that currently almost every company has a variety of agreements (Gilroy, 1993; Inkpen, 1996). Due to the number and complexity of the relationships in a network, it is difficult to clearly distinguish which company is a competitor and which is a cooperative partner, because usually they are both. Thus, it would be better to refer to cooperative competition as an economic survival strategy. Cooperation and competition make up both sides of the same coin; they coexist.

Companies swing between cooperation and competition when they let themselves become involved in the latent uncontrollability of cooperative agreements. However, their perspective of action is formed by a limited rationality. Economic action in a decision area formed by uncertainty is only possible if the partners mutually trust each other so that a hermeneutic circulation of knowledge can take place. If knowledge is purposely released to the cooperative partners for internalization and thus opportunistic behavior is given up, coevolution of knowledge can set in.

Limited Rationalism and Trust

In a world of perfect foresight, economic actions would be nothing more than mechanical and automatic selections, oriented along logically fixed operations. The goal of economic action would be based on the underlying assumption that individual behavior is mostly led by self-interest and that all economic incidents can thus be traced back to the individual's behavior. This idea, which can be traced back to the model world of neoclassic theory, states that an individual who is limited in possibilities of action chooses that alternative from the limited possibilities that best corresponds to his or her interests (Simon, 1983). This presupposes that an individual is capable of aligning a logical order of preference of all possible alternatives which then can be represented as commonly effective functions. Through this ascertainment the choice takes on a mathematical formula and becomes subject to a rigorous analysis in which the decision for the best possible alternative is sought to maximize these useful functions under the given circumstances.

The neoclassic theory, next to the goal of maximizing usefulness, employs a type of thinking that can be classified as universal. In the process of installing a converging system, the diversity of competitive structures is replaced by a single dominating economic structure. Culturally different opinions that exist about economic actions are thus often denied to neutralize the economic focus of the company.

Actions as a repetition of converted decisions always take place, as Simon (1961) has shown, in the context of an uncertainty caused by natural order and limited by cultural diversity. Making a decision is a creative act, unleashed by the freedom of the formation of unforeseen hypotheses. With this background, companies come up with different evaluations of situations and develop different action strategies from these, even when they rely on the best available evidence.

The selection of action alternatives is carried out under the premises of a bounded rationality of the companies (Simon, 1983). Receiving and processing knowledge to find a solution takes time and is costly. Companies intend to act rationally, but their rationality holds certain limitations due to the time and energy needed to take in knowledge and process it. To manage the complex decision, the companies rely on simplified decisional rules and processes. Because of such thoughts, companies tend to look for satisfactory solutions, not optimal ones. In contrast to optimal solutions, satisfactory solutions are limited to realizing a minimal level. Most human decisions, whether individual or made in an organization, are led by the desire to find and select satisfactory solutions. Only in exceptional cases do decision makers seek optimal alternatives.

Bounded rationality and opportunism of the individual actors are assumed to be essential sources of transaction costs. In this sense, bounded rationality means that individuals intend to be rational but their calculating and choosing capacities are finite, bounded. This implies that incomplete information about opportunities results in limited ability to predict the future. Assuming omniscience is unrealistic; people do not know everything, so they make mistakes. Opportunism follows from bounded rationality plus self-interest. Opportunistic people pursue their self-interest with guile. If it is profitable, people will lie or cheat. Assuming strict honesty is unrealistic.

The decision whether cooperation between companies should be chosen in a network setting or antagonistic isolation when it comes to competitive relationships, is, according to Killing (1988), inherently uncertain. If the strategy of cooperative competition is chosen, then the company must be aware of the loss of control over its knowledge potentials. Risk is always associated with cooperatives. Possibly, the partner companies are capable of learning more quickly than the company itself. This could lead to a company in a cooperative network becoming obsolete, since it is no longer useful to the partners. Also, the loss of knowledge to third parties cannot be completely controlled. Japanese companies have been especially successful in the past, as most studies about this topic have shown (Reich and Mankin, 1986; Jones and Shill, 1991; Richter and Vettel, 1995). They come out of cooperation agreements with Western companies strengthened, while the competitive ability of the Western partner decreased or at least remained at the initial starting level. Even if the interests and knowledge potentials are initially equal, a greater advantage to the Japanese partner starts appearing over time.

This makes clear that many uncertain factors are a part of network cooperations. On the other hand, cooperative competition in strategic networks always yields immense chances and growth potential that would not even be considered in a noncooperative. In this sense, the past competitive strategy is the safer solution because it shows, at least briefly, a secured economic scope of action. The possible spectrum between controlling possibilities and chances is pictured in Figure 2.7.

An optimal solution for the choice of an economic action alternative would probably be to have a high degree of future possibilities without having to take risks. This solution, however, is not workable since none of the traditional competitive strategies offer comparable development paths to the cooperative competition strategies. The cooperative competition strategies, on the other hand, are risky if the partners do not trust one another. The literature on cooperations between companies indicates trust as the most important decision criterion for a successful cooperation (Killing, 1988; Kogut, 1988).

Cooperation must always be based on trust. It would not be right to accuse the partner of purposely copying or trying to protect his own knowledge potential by treating it like a "black box." Such

FIGURE 2.7. Perception of Action Alternatives

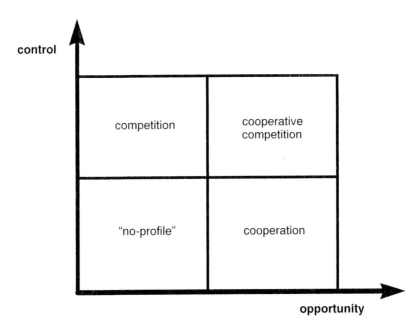

behavior would ultimately disturb the atmosphere of cooperation and would be disrespectful to the partner. In Japan trust does not have to explicitly be mentioned; it is inherent. In the West, however, when the relationship between supplier and buyer is taking place through the market, buyers have an incentive to play their suppliers against one another to achieve the best price or best quality. Suppliers do not like to reveal information about costs or patented production sequences since they fear that the information will be used against them. If suppliers can realize returns or learning curve effects, they would rather keep the profit to themselves than to pass it along to their customers.

The companies bound together in a strategic network are dependent on one another and on an acceptable cooperation. The more a relationship is designed for the long run, the more the interests will converge and the higher the level of trust will be in the reciprocity of the relationship (Fukuyama, 1995). The permanence of a relationship combined with a high level of consistency in personnel improves the mutual understanding and the atmosphere of interaction. This leaves the network organization more flexible in competition since changes that affect everyone can be carried out more quickly and easily. Access to critical resources and the binding into a collective strategy are reasons why companies are willing to accept rules upon entrance into a network organization, although this network organization will limit their individual freedom of action compared to a single market. Since the entire network association becomes more efficient through these rules, they allow the long-term economic survival of the established and institutionally anchored member companies as a kind of reward.

Hermeneutic Circulation

The term hermeneutic stems from Hermes, who was the messenger of the gods in Greek mythology. His job was to translate the wishes of the gods into earthly interests and communicate them to humans. Aristotle used the principle of hermeneutics in philosophical questions whereby the understanding of human existence in the sense of metaphysics was foremost. Hermeneutics as a science was born out of the necessity to interpret the Bible. The word of God needed interpretation to make its meaning more obvious to a larger circle of readers and listeners.

In the late nineteenth century, hermeneutics expanded into a general methodology that was to be effective as the basis for the humanities. Hermeneutics became the scientific method for not only the interpretation of texts, but human actions and social behavior in general (Phillips, 1987). In contrast to the less exact measurable phenomena of the sciences, human actions are always relative to the standpoint of observers, who have the ability to interpret a fact by integrating past personal experiences. New interpretations become part of the existing knowledge drawn from experiences, so that human knowledge, just as much as ethical value models, is subject to a steady evolution. Personal knowledge drawn from experiences is reflected in all of the accessible human knowledge, so that the evolution of knowledge occurs in the interaction corridor of individual and general accessible knowledge. This process is also referred to as a *hermeneutic circle* (Gadamer, 1977).

The accumulation of knowledge is one of the underlying motives for companies to become part of cooperatives in the form of networks. Knowledge necessary for the realization of a certain company goal may be supplied in this way. Casson (1990) called the accumulation of knowledge in cooperative agreements "internalization." Knowledge of the partner is instilled into the organization little by little and linked with existing knowledge, whereby learning of different orders is used. Casson points out that cooperatives are usually sought in an egocentric manner and that partners often purposely play out one another by keeping acquired knowledge a secret. If a business goal can be reached with less expense with one cooperative than with another, it is possible to switch from one cooperative agreement to another.

According to Casson, internalization of knowledge is a typical example of opportunistic economic behavior and of the utilization of power resulting from different levels of freedom for the involved. The accumulation of knowledge is seen as a one-sided attempt to enrich oneself and to secure a dominant position in the network association. Internalization negates the interactive component of a mutual evolution between the giving and taking organizational unit.

The principle of internalization is set against the process of hermeneutic circulation. This takes effect when a gap exists between organizational and nonorganizational knowledge. The gap can be overcome by using the hermeneutic interpretation of internal and foreign knowledge. This process is based on the proper fitting of cooperative partners into the higher coevolution. Next to the internalization of knowledge, a process called externalization sets in. Organizationally internal knowledge is presented to the partner for internalization. After a partner has taken in the external knowledge and processed it, it is in turn set free for the internalization of other companies. Hermeneutic circulation, purposely presented by all partners, is thus a balance of internalization and externalization of knowledge. With this, hermeneutic circulation learning processes of first, second, or third order can occur. In the context of a cooperative competition, hermeneutic circulation takes on the form shown in Figure 2.8.

In the first step, a company externalizes knowledge into the network, where it is integrated through cooperative agreements. The external knowledge can be in the form of innovations, competencies, and cultural behavioral norms. In the network the knowledge is intrinsically enriched by the cooperative partners with the

FIGURE 2.8. Hermeneutic Circulation

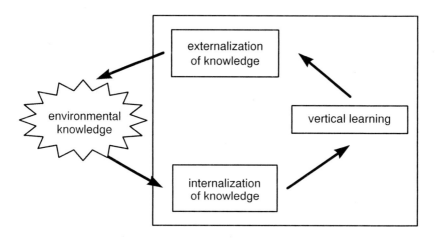

existing knowledge components and is finally returned to the company. In the next step the company internalizes the knowledge enriched in this fashion. The internalization is the result of an intentional, systematic search for knowledge, which can be of advantage to the evolution of its internal knowledge base. In the further process of hermeneutic circulation, the internalized knowledge continues to develop through vertical learning processes. After a period of knowledge consolidation from the internal organization, it can then be at the disposal of the network association.

Hermeneutic circulation thus results from positive feedback between a company and its network environment and is in accord with the tradition of theories about organizational learning. Organizational learning is, as discussed previously, a process that changes and uses the knowledge base of a company (Hedberg, 1981; Walsh and Ungson, 1991). Beyond the change and utilization of an individual's base of knowledge, hermeneutic circulation is a process through which the knowledge base of an organizational environment can be changed in a positive way.

Organizational learning must be assumed as the basis of cooperative competition, because it is the point of reference for all interactions between companies. The famous "always has been this way" contains the basic idea of modern hermeneutics: in any communication process we always have to make assumptions. We stand on the shoulders of those who have communicated before us.

Coevolution of Knowledge

Evolution usually refers to the development to a higher state of a system that is better than the original state (Adams, 1991). This insight is based on Darwin's evolution theory in which according to the principle of natural breeding, more and more adaptable species evolve. Natural systems continuously develop and leave the survival of developmental specifics behind them.

Variation, selection, and retention as the basic processes of Darwin's evolution theory are also central processes of Hannan and Freeman's Population Ecology approach (Hannan and Freeman, 1989). Their central idea is that companies, depending on their fitting into the environment, are either positively or negatively selected. Darwin's law of selection is projected onto organizations.

According to the variation processes, network cooperatives develop like all organizational forms, as a result of economic actions. The trigger for the selection is a poor fit between company and environment. An adaptation of the companies or cooperative concept becomes necessary to diminish the poor fit and thus to forgo the selection. The process of retention takes care of the preservation, duplication, and reproduction of organizational forms.

Critics of the population ecology approach (compare, e.g., Richter and Teramoto, 1996) point out that network cooperatives are based on trust between partners and that Darwinistic selection mechanisms can only unsatisfactorily explain the complexity of network cooperatives. A social Darwinism no longer seems to fit into the modern landscape of strategic networks. Cooperative competition demands that companies give up their antagonistic behavior and begin to coordinate their activities. The companies expand their perceived horizon beyond their own organizational boundaries through a consciously pursued hermeneutic circulation. With this, they differentiate themselves from those companies that are not part of the network association. They do not run through the close evolutionary circle of selection, but develop their knowledge potential mutually with their cooperative partners.

If two or more organizations link together and evolve mutually, the result could be better than if each organization evolves on its own. Hermeneutic circulation carried out by more than one organization shall therefore be referred to as "coevolution of knowledge" to emphasize the melting of singular company surroundings into a network association. As shown in Figure 2.9, hermeneutically bound companies mutually achieve a real advance in the development of knowledge potentials accessible to anyone.

Companies and the respective network association together reach quality growth of existing knowledge potentials (k_1 in comparison to k_0). Coevolution of knowledge is a recursively set-in, historical process along a subjectively felt time axis (t_1 in comparison to t_0), whereby the evolutionary process—as opposed to revolutionary innovation in the sense of a *eureka* effect—is carried out mostly in increments.

Teramoto and Iwasaki (1991) describe the coevolution of companies in strategic networks as a mechanism to produce synergies. The

FIGURE 2.9. Coevolution of Knowledge

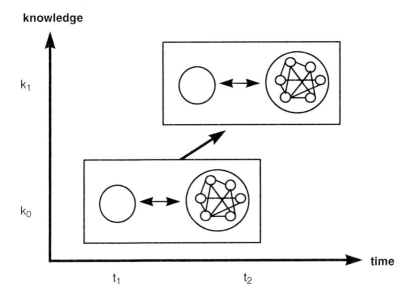

exchange of knowledge is directed multilaterally and company functions are synergistically fused. Organizations and their environments are engaged in a pattern of synergistic coevolution, in which each produces the other. Just as in nature, the environment of an organism is composed of other organisms. Organizational environments are in large measure composed of other organizations. And once we recognize this, it becomes clear that organizations are in principle able to influence the nature of their environment. They can play an active role in shaping their future, especially when acting in concert with other organizations. Environments then always become negotiated environments to some extent, rather than independent external forces.

Coevolution of knowledge can rely on several companies as promoters for the creation of knowledge. Depending on the necessary counterbalance, one of the companies cooperating in the strategic network takes over the leading role and drives the evolutionary system forward by externalizing knowledge and doing real preliminary work. The knowledge potential of companies increases through constant competition with one another, or put differently, they are subject to a dynamic feedback due to their imbalance of internalization and externalization.

Chapter 3

Driving Forces
of Strategic Networks

Cooperation and the coordination of work between companies are topics that a line of Nobel prize winners such as Kenneth Arrow, Ronald Coase, and George Stigler have tried to tackle on a scientific level. Historically, cooperation—under many different names—has increasingly gained importance as a topic of research, especially since the second half of the 1980s. Essentially, however, one still speaks of a theory deficit in the area of cooperations (e.g., in Gilroy, 1993; Inkpen, 1996; Dunning, 1997), because various ideas such as the transaction cost idea by Williamson, which is increasingly becoming a focal point, only explain partial areas and are still not yet developed. A commonly accepted "cooperation theory" for the explanation of the multilevel effect mechanisms does not exist.

The goal of this chapter is to fundamentally develop the phenomenon of cooperation between companies and to make it transparent on the basis of theoretical explanations. At the beginning of each section, an idea will be presented that illuminates a specific part from the reality of cooperation between companies. In detail these are the system, growth, and game theories. Building onto these ideas, experiences from real life and theory will be highlighted and illustrated with examples of Japanese companies. Furthermore, the experiences will be sublimated under specific effect mechanisms that can also be interpreted as driving forces of strategic networks. These driving forces are *permeability, autopoiesis,* and *symbiosis.*

Permeability is a concept from systems theory. It states that organizations are neither completely closed off nor completely open toward their environment. They require life-essential resources from the environment and make channels to internalize the resources. At the same time, signals to the environment are sent through the channels. Permeability shows up as a partial opening of the corporate system in light of the integration of a closed-off organizational unit (individual company) into a higher unit (strategic network).

Autopoiesis is an aspect of the constructivistic cognition theory, which tries to understand the organization of living systems in regard to its uniform character. With this, living organisms are given a sort of autonomy that goes far beyond common ideas of self-reliance and independence, yet the intensity and the number of links between living organisms and their environment are more radically emphasized than before. The comparison of networks to living organisms arises, since cooperative agreements are always, by definition, in a state of change (Richter and Teramoto, 1996). The strategic resources bound into a cooperative agreement cannot be completely controlled by the cooperative partners. Thus, they change the platform of future cooperation potentials, depending on past use and translation. Autopoietic systems constantly produce their own circular organization that is kept constant as a basic size. Because of their circular organization, living systems are self-referential and in reference to their organization, homeostatic systems are autonomic toward their environment.

The third driving force, symbiosis, which is similar to the concepts of permeability and autopoiesis, is an idea that was originally developed in biology. Based on their sequential interactions, two or more living systems are bound symbiotically. Their corresponding structures then experience sequential changes without destroying the identity of the original systems. From a symbiotic link of two or more organisms a consensual area results in which structurally certain conditional changes in the linked organisms have to be matched with one another. In doing so, an organism sacrifices its optimal adaptation for a short time, but ends up receiving more in the long run than it has originally given. Similar to living organisms, cooperating companies free up certain resources for internalization, but at the same time receive access to resources of the partner. At best, not only a mere resource exchange occurs, but the resources are linked and further developed by one another, so that the companies eventually achieve real evolutionary advantages.

The three driving forces of strategic networks also include structural and dynamic aspects for the interim business organization. A moment is a statistical excerpt of an evolutionary sequence that is capable of connecting in a time frame and is thus dynamic. The dynamics of strategic networks show up in the inherent change of the cooperative relationship and the changing attitudes of the cooperative partners about one another. The relationship of the participants of the cooperative thus is often compared to a situation similar to marriage and the cooperative is often seen as the "child" of this relationship (Lorange and Ross, 1992). Especially for network cooperations, terms such as "marriages," "aging of the relationship" and "divorces" are often used, but the term "second spring" is also quite common. The entire process of "networking" is of immense importance for the evolution of relationships between cooperatives. The aspects of permeability, autopoiesis, and symbiosis lead the way from a focus on contingency and structure to an explanation for the dynamics of strategic networks.

PERMEABILITY

Japanese companies generally neither close themselves off to their environment, with which they have a competing relationship, nor pursue a continuous cooperation strategy. The boundaries are, as Teramoto (1990) notices, permeable, which means they can be penetrated. Competition can promote a network system and cooperation, on the other hand, can stimulate competition.

The permeability of the Japanese economic system in general and of strategic networks in particular, shows in the way that Japanese companies take outside influences, like new product technologies, and combine them with existing knowledge to generate knowledge superior to the original product technology (Fransman, 1990). It would thus be incorrect to simply accuse the Japanese of "copying." They could however, viewed from a cultural historical point, be accused of copying as early as the seventh century by taking over cultural artifact ideas from China. Later, at the beginning of the Meiji reforms starting in 1868, with the opening toward the West, they could be accused of copying from the West as well. During the reforms initiated during the reign of Prince Shotoku (593-622), Buddhism, Confucianism, ideas about imperialism, art styles such as Indian ink drawings, scientific discoveries, building of cities, and architecture poured into the country. Even many Japanese don't know that the *kimono*, the original Japanese formal gown for ladies, stems from the Chinese Tang dynasty, which was forgotten in China but survived in a changed form in Japan. The Chinese culture, back then indisputably the most developed and so-phisticated in the world, changed the simple Japanese farmers' society over the course of two centuries into a society that was comparable to that of the Chinese. Something similar occurred at the end of the nineteenth century, whereby industrialization, science and technology, and the judicial system of the Americans and Europeans were more sought after than their art, religions, and philosophies.

These two unprecedented takeovers of foreign ideas gave the Japanese the reputation of imitators, as Hoyt (1991) points out, but probably unjustly because foreign ideas were not simply copied. It is not the fact that Japan opened itself to China in ancient times and to the West in modern times that makes those events singular and remarkable, but rather the Japanese ability to melt foreign ideas into their own traditions and adapt them to their own needs that marks their true mastery. Despite their modern appearance, the Japanese are still an ultraconservative society. Although open to foreign in-fluences, they have never given up their own traditions. Instead, they apply new ideas without discarding the old, so that they end up pulling their energy from the same old roots, despite many changes.

Examples of the combination of new ideas with tradition are the adoption of Buddhism while retaining Shintoism as the old Japa-nese belief, the adoption of the Chinese characters with the devel-opment of two-syllable alphabets, and the adoption of the idea of the emperor. Regarding the latter example, the Japanese changed the concept of the Son of Heaven in one important point: every Chinese emperor needed a mandate from heaven, a godly blessing that could be denied or revoked. The Japanese did not adopt this mandate, because it contradicted the Shintoistic idea of the godly origin of the emperor house: not an order from God, but an authen-tic descendancy from God.

While contradictions and defense mechanisms inevitably develop in the West, whether they are closings or, following resignation, openings, the Japanese are capable of building bridges. In this way tradition is never displaced by the modern; whatever is added goes on top. The boundaries between old and new, outside and inside, *uchi* and *soto*, are flexible. Similar to the cultural historical connection between old and new, Japanese companies behave within strategic networks. New information that is mediated by a cooperative partner is combined with existing competencies. The original skills are not thrown overboard to adapt to the new partner company. Numagami, Ohta, and Nonaka (1996) conclude from this that permeability is a basic quality of Japanese companies that contributes toward competitive advantage.

The idea of permeability goes back to the theory of systems, which tries to explain the characteristics of the system boundary as an essential part of a system.

Basics of Systems Theory

Every system has many elements that are in noticeable relation to one another. The concept of "system" implies that the relationship among these elements is tighter than the relationship between the elements and the environment. This constitutes a difference, a boundary between the elements and the environment. Only in regard to this difference are systems more than the sum of their parts. It is this difference that is consciously, or unconsciously, seen as an advantage by the elements of the system. This means that it is advantageous or even necessary for the elements to maintain this difference.

The concept of "system" has been described in various ways. Since Von Bertalanffy (1962) founded the systems theory, different criteria have been discussed that differentiate a system from a "non-system," or which developmental levels a system can achieve. In Figure 3.1, the variety of possible systems is divided into the three types—open, closed, and permeable—and is discussed based on implicit world perception, perception of the environment, and time perception.

FIGURE 3.1. Closed, Open, and Permeable Systems

	closed system	open system	permeable system
world perception	mechanics	theory of relativity	self-organization
perception of environment	does not exist	environment structures system	system structures environment
perception of time	static	dynamic	irreversible

Newton taught that the world can be explained with the help of mechanics. With physics as the guiding science, an event in nature could be described with the help of simple formulas. Natural phenomena are thus linked in a linear fashion and strictly determinable. The world according to Newton is that of a mechanically functioning engine in which all processes can seemingly work trouble free. Such a reductionism limits the complex world to simple movement equations. According to this worldview, the world is a closed system that reacts to guidance commands but has no power of its own. Any influences that differ from guiding measures are registered as disturbances for which there are no preprogrammed answers. Closed systems are always in a static balance. Changing balances or even states far from a balance are negated.

At the beginning of the century, physics was revolutionized by Einstein's theory of relativity. The theory of relativity includes the linkage of space and time and explains how forces can spread out over space and time. Discontinuities of nature are also excepted. The induced picture of humans perceives the human in the functional variety of natural surroundings. The exchange of energy leads to a dynamic systems equilibrium (homeostasis), a state that lends open systems an action potential to maintain their internal order. The goal of open systems is survival in the environment, for which growth is an important criterion. In comparison to closed systems, open ones are capable of living.

Since the early 1960s, ideas started to develop in different scientific areas that tried to explain instabilities and spontaneously occurring processes of order. These ideas were later termed "self-organization." Evolution beyond thermodynamic equilibrium is seen as possible. Instabilities are more often the rule; stable system conditions are the exception. A permeable system, in comparison to open systems, does not have input-output relationship with its environment, but actively structures its environment through recursive feedback. Complexity is purposely sought, not reduced or conserved, through the system's internal structuring event and is due to interactions with the environment. Permeable systems reproduce their unity, structures, and elements in a continuous, operatively closed, but environmentally open and thus permeable process with the elements of which they are composed.

In contrast to physical systems, the boundaries of social systems, like strategic networks of cooperating companies, cannot be physically/spatially grasped, but are symbolically determined. As Luhmann (1995) suggests, social systems can question the meaning of their actions. Economic organizations as social systems, whether they are individual companies or strategic networks, continue to write a certain story and determine by their history which actions are useful to them and which are not. By doing so they legitimate their staking of boundaries between the areas to be included in the layout. Social systems do not automatically form in the course of social differentiation, but their development depends on the logic and dynamic of the decisional behavior in organizations.

Companies as a social system can take on the shape of a closed, open, or permeable system. Only permeable system organizations are capable of forming cooperative relationships, since they have an interactive connection to the environment. The primary goal is not the exchange of goods and knowledge but the development of a mutual social identity. Aburdene (1999) defines self-organization and the underlying structure of permeable systems as the business megatrend of the twenty-first century. The cooperating companies go through a socialization process in which no special norms, cognition, behavioral patterns, or other data are transferred from the outside to the inside, but in which they first have to form in sequential interactions between the participating companies.

The resulting strategic network is constituted as a social system, just like the cooperating individual companies. Companies can create their own environments, and thus the surrounding social structure, through interaction with other companies. This structure contains mutually perceived meaningful parameters that separate the strategic network from its environment. The network boundary, depending on its meaning, can be closed, open, or permeable.

Networks Between Market and Hierarchy

Strategic networks are a strategic option positioned between market and hierarchy. The market is the most open economic organizational form imaginable. Hierarchy, on the other hand, is a closed organizational form, concerned with the boundary between inside and outside (Powell, 1990). In the market transaction, independent companies draw up a selling contract, in which purely objective criteria such as price, quality, etc., determine the coming about of a market transaction. As a prime example of market transactions, the exchanging economic subjects on the organized stock market usually remain anonymous.

In the hierarchy as an economic organizational form, several or all transaction processes can occur within the same company. In it, the coordination of the transformation process is given to a higher institution and uniform leadership. While objective criteria carry out the central coordination function in the market transaction, an authoritarian behavior commands in the hierarchy. An example of a hierarchy organization is the merger and acquisition of two competitors under the roof of a central controlling authority.

In a network association, the mutual trust the companies have toward one another works as a transaction mechanism and to strengthen cooperation relationships. Price and behavioral instructions also work, but in a weakened form. In Figure 3.2, the options of network cooperations in an area of conflict between market and hierarchy are classified.

The increasing desirability of cooperations between companies stems from the failure of pure market mechanisms and the insufficiency of hierarchical forms of cooperation (Teece, 1981; Imai and Itami, 1988). Economic change and the compulsion for more flexibility that arises from it challenges companies to desegregate certain activities and to externalize corporate functions. The need for more coordination and integration of activities that arises from this demands an efficient management of the relationships between companies.

FIGURE 3.2. Market, Network, Hierarchy

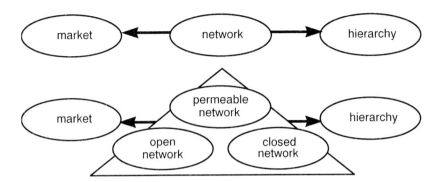

The fitting of the network between market and hierarchy goes back to the transaction cost approach of Williamson (1975, 1985). Williamson believes that a transaction takes place if a good or a service is transferred over an organizational interface. Transaction costs refer to the friction of transfer. This means the costs for information gathering, for negotiations, for the navigation and control of the transaction, and for the necessary adaptive changes. The amount of the transaction costs determines the optimal organizational form. From the theoretical transaction perspective, strategic networks are seen as a hybrid form of organization of economic exchange processes, which contain both elements of exchange in the market as well as in the hierarchy. The transaction costs within strategic networks are seen as potentially low if environmental uncertainties exist. In his transaction cost theory, Williamson believes that work sharing processes can be coordinated within a continuum, with the market at one end and the hierarchy at the other end. Transaction costs decide which organizational form to choose. Companies, or rather individuals within the company, evaluate transaction costs of alternative organizational forms and choose the option that can minimize transaction costs.

A transaction involves the process of initiation, agreement, control and, if necessary, adaptation of exchange services. Transaction costs refer to all costs that arise in connection with the gathering and processing of information, with the negotiation processes, the specification of agreements, the supervision, and if necessary, the carrying out of sanctions. The total amount of transaction cost is determined by the uncertainty under which the transaction occurs and by the frequency with which it occurs. Williamson claims that the more troublesome and thus the more expensive organizational form of cooperation is more useful to reduce transaction costs in the long run than market and hierarchy transactions.

According to the transaction cost theory, market transactions fail in transactions that have a high degree of uncertainty and complexity. Hierarchies, however, are more likely to fail with certain transactions of low complexity. In organizations structured by hierarchy, adaptation is costly. This means that costs for the change of the organization accrue. Intermediate organizational forms between market and hierarchy, on the other hand, can combine the advantages of both organizational forms.

The company as a network of contracts is the starting point for the agency theory, which asks how a contract relationship between a principal and an agent can be optimized (Eisenhardt, 1989). Both contract partners follow their own interests and try to maximize their individual benefits. The principal is interested in as high an output as possible as a result of the actions of the agent, while the agent is interested in achieving the output with as low an expenditure as possible. Strategic networks are seen as intertwined multilevel agency relationships. The agency theory can be seen as a special variant of the transaction idea, which has the goal to coordinate and manage opposite interests.

The concept of strategic networks as interfirm organizations is linked to transaction costs and agency relationships. Imai and Itami (1988) describe networks as organizational forms between internal organizations and the market, which are constituted by an intertwining reciprocal relationship. Networks are not a homogeneous form of organization, but rather a mixture of strong and weak relationships between companies, whose special advantages lie in the fact that their link can always change depending on the needs of the environment.

By fitting it into a vacuum between market and hierarchy, three forms of strategic networks can be seen, which along the systems theory, always portray a different environmental understanding: open, permeable, and closed networks.

Open networks are closest to the market. The entrance and exit barriers are limited and the degree of mutual dependency stays relatively low, although links in the form of multilateral trust develop. The Japanese trans-*keiretsu* cooperative, e.g., the *igyoushu koryu*, are "open," according to their characteristics and functional mechanisms. Although open networks create a natural focus and internal synergy for leveraging knowledge, they can be detrimental to monitoring knowledge development outside the firm. One of the solutions to this is to locate in industrial districts such as the Silicon Valley, and create a natural environment for intellectual synergy. Associations tend to develop that foster the exchange of generalized as opposed to firm-specific knowledge. Unlike the United States where these associations are more or less spontaneous developments and limited to fostering the exchange of generalized knowledge, associations in Japan are linked with government agencies and are much more active in developing new technology and promoting joint research projects.

Closed networks, on the other hand, are closest to hierarchies. Usually a focal company holds a net of cooperative relationships directed into the company. Traditional forms of cooperation in Japan, especially the production networks, represent this type of network. It is evident that the strength of network affiliations can become so rigid over time that the primary advantages of networks over corporate ownership—i.e., flexibility, adaptability, and openness to informational environments— are impaired. Because organizations can devote energy and attention to only so many relationships, the stronger the ties, the fewer the number of ties, and the slower the diffusion of communication through the network; thus "the strength of weak ties" (Granovetter, 1973). The loss of network flexibility and adaptability and its consequences are rarely salient during times of growth and prosperity, but become painfully evident in the face of adversity and cathartic change.

Permeable networks take on an intermediate role. They are especially known for being interlocked with other networks. Two or more networks constitute the environment and communicate with one another: Such "intertwined" networks describe a logic of second order, because the cooperating companies of one network work as a whole with companies that cooperate with a different network. A permeable network is a type of strategic network that has evolved in Japan since the early 1990s. This will be shown in the following case example.

We are not trying to advocate for permeable networks based on stringent evidence with transaction costs. This must be left for the transaction cost theorizers. All three organizational forms between market and hierarchy prove to be efficient organizational forms under certain conditions. Recently, however, an empirical move from open and closed networks toward permeable networks is evident, thus we shall discuss the obvious advantages of this organizational form with the help of a case example.

Case Example: Toyota

It is interesting to note that Japan's prolonged economic depression is causing stress within its network structures. The principal role in providing key network resources such as finance, marketing, and technology was played by the large "parent" companies at the center of each (closed) production network and its affiliated banks and financial institutions. The Japanese automotive industry, like most of the other industries, is in a process of adapting to a new stage of development. After a phase of steady growth until the end of the 1980s, Japan is seeing signs that growth can be limited. Many Japanese automobile firms had to face tremendous turnover losses in the 1990s and some manufacturers such as Mazda, Subaru, and Isuzu are confronted with a shrinking process that, according to Itami (1994) and Banerji and Sambharya (1996), can be dangerous. The European and American automotive industries, which were previously depressed, are in the process of recovering.

The crisis of the Japanese automobile manufacturers affects their relationship with suppliers. The crisis also hits the suppliers, since they can no longer sell their products the way they used to. Consequently, the Japanese automobile manufacturers have begun to experiment with new supplier structures. The vertical cooperation between automobile manufacturer and supplier is currently being redefined in Japan and being expanded beyond its original meaning (Abo, 1995).

Since the beginning of the 1990s, Toyota, as the most famous representative of vertically organized production networks, has started to reorient its supplier and production structures. The reorientation essentially consists of three points (Nishiguchi, 1993).

Toyota took measures to decrease the extreme dependency of its supplier firms. Traditionally, an essential feature of the supply relationships in Japan, and the one that has been the prime object of scholarly inquiry among Japanese Marxist economists, is said to be the exploitative nature of the relationship between the customer firm and the supplier. Marxist scholars discuss monopoly capital exploiting smaller supplier firms (Sako, 1992). As far as Toyota is concerned, suppliers were recently asked to also supply competing firms. Companies of their own production networks were given the target to make 30 percent of their turnover with competing firms such as Nissan, Mitsubishi Motors, or Honda. Toyota and Nissan, the number one and two firms of the Japanese automobile industry, now purchase parts and components from suppliers of the competitors. Both firms had so far followed the strategy to distance themselves from each other and to avoid potential cooperation agreements. Nippondenso, Toyota's biggest supplier, now already supplies most other Japanese automobile manufacturers, particularly Nissan.

Toyota further began to examine its production network with the goal to remove all redundancies in the manufacturing and delivery process. Suppliers were asked to examine any possibilities of bilateral cooperation, even to the point of merger. Some smaller firms of the Toyota group have indeed taken the route of merger, so that the number of active supplying firms has decreased. The approach of the supplying firms is such that firms of different production networks have bound together for a partial cooperative. For example, Toyota's Koyo Seiko entered an R&D cooperation with Atsugi Yunisha, a firm of the Nissan group, in the area of power steering elements.

Toyota also asks its suppliers to expand in technology fields that have no direct connection with the automobile industry. Shiroki Kogyo, a manufacturer of automobile doors, diversified into solar technology. The automobile suppliers either follow the strategy of start-ups on their own or of cooperation with existing companies.

As a consequence of this measure, the production structures that have so far been an important success factor for Toyota disintegrate for the benefit of more flexible models. With the new order more market closeness and better cost structures are expected. Toyota has taken the weaknesses of its own model that has been copied by many American and European companies in the process of benchmarking and tried to dissolve the rigid association of the vertical production *keiretsu* for the benefit of more flexible structures. Toyota is moving in the direction of a permeable network in which the inside orientation, which has always been felt necessary for innovation and efficiency (e.g., Womack, Jones, and Ross, 1990), is being discarded for the benefit of cooperative exchange relationships with other manufacturers and their suppliers. The production network of Toyota now cooperates in its entirety with the production networks of Nissan, Mitsubishi Motors, Honda, etc. Behind this new orientation is the idea that exaggerated dependencies between automobile manufacturers and suppliers must be avoided to decrease susceptibility of the production system in times of crisis. It is more important to have a high degree of permeability that can give rise to manufacturers and suppliers alike.

The model of the permeable network fits, according to its character, between the models of the open and closed networks (see Figure 3.3). The closed network represents the traditional form of cooperative in a vertically organized production association between Japanese automobile manufacturers and their suppliers. This model gives efficiency advantages so long as the supplying company has no scale economies and if a temporary widening of capacities becomes desired. It is also advantageous if their own capital link should or has to be limited (Monden, 1991). From the perspective of the contractor, the system helps secure sales, availability of expertise, and possibly lends support during times of crisis. It should be said that the single production networks are autonomous and are not dependent on obtaining achievements with companies of other production networks.

The model of open networks is favored by Western companies. Although the automobile firms usually prefer to work with certain suppliers, and thus distance themselves from an industrial achieve-

FIGURE 3.3. Strategic Networks in the Automobile Industry

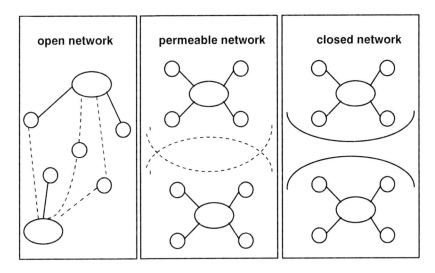

ment construct in a free and autonomous market, they take the liberty to be able to change suppliers on demand. Since the worldwide crisis in the automobile industry in 1993, European automobile manufacturers began a rigorous cost management program that was initially passed on to the suppliers. Company strategists, such as Volkswagen purchase manager Ignacio Lopez, played suppliers against one another to reduce the material costs. The large European supplier companies such as Bosch, Lukas, and Valeo are consequently independent of large firms so that their client market power is not limited.

The prototype of permeable networks has developed from the Japanese model of the closed network. Due to increasingly complex production processes and products, the automobile manufacturers are interested in competent contractors. The limited technical ability to absorb technology, the output quality, and out-of-date capital stock were the main problems in the early 1990s in the supply industry. Many supplier companies, partially supported by the automobile industry, try to increase their competitive ability in the various segments of a widened technological landscape. On top of this, the single production networks of the automobile industry are beginning to be linked together. Networks as a whole are starting to interact. The view of the permeable network is therefore more appropriate for the automobile industry than the old scenarios of dependency.

AUTOPOIESIS

The Edo and the Meiji periods—the years between 1600 and 1912—due to their changes, offered the basis from which the *zaibatsu* could develop. In the raw material industry, the development of companies with monopolylike characters increased conspicuously within these 300 years. Family-owned firms such as Mitsubishi, Mitsui, Sumitomo, and Yasuda (today: Fuyo-*keiretsu*), to name the four most important, grew substantially to include the most important industries as well as trade and finance. This growth caused an organic change from retail trade to a structure in which a family holding (*honsha*) reigned over a variety of companies of different businesses through kinship connections and exclusive stockholdership. The history of Japanese network companies is marked by relatively few structural breaks (Odagiri, 1992; Fruin, 1992) and usually happened along organic developmental strategies. Organic growth could be used as an explanatory model for the sense of tradition of Japanese society in general and the homogeneity of Japanese society specifically.

The economic development from an agricultural state to a leading industrial state occurred with phenomenal speed. A quickly growing home market and limited resources demanded entrepreneurial behavior that could satisfy these requirements. To strive for growth similar to Western companies through wide production lines or through internalization of all production levels would not have been a suitable strategy in light of such requirements. It was accepted to take risks, to be technologically creative, and to make leading-edge decisions. However, to increase capacities and personnel for this would have required substantial money and abilities (Makino, 1985; Fruin, 1992). These were often only available in limited amounts. The path taken by the Japanese, to achieve growth through cooperation in production and distribution, allowed a decrease in risk, combined with flexibility and access to the resources of the partner firms.

In Chapter 2, we discussed the idea of coevolution of knowledge as the result of hermeneutic circulation. Companies exchange their knowledge potentials in the network association and develop along a mutually pursued cooperative goal. In doing so, not only do their knowledge potentials evolve, but inevitably also the organizational structures of the companies. As a sign of further diversification, they can grow according to the number of their employees, the turnover, and the number of business units. These explicit determinants of the business evolution reflect the hermeneutic growth in knowledge. It is clear that companies can develop their own basic strategies on how the future development is to occur. This way companies can enter, according to the idea of specific competitive advantage (Porter, 1980), an alcove strategy in a certain business or a global diversification, etc. Of special importance for the future company evolution is, as Alic et al. (1992) stressed, the decision whether future growth should be achieved by merger and acquisition or through the finding of one's own internal organizational competencies, combined with thoughtout cooperation strategies.

A growth structure that was developed in the field of science in past years is that of autopoiesis. The colorful word autopoiesis (Greek. *autos* = self; *poiesis* = make, create) was formed by the Chilean neurobiologist Humberto Maturana, who used this to characterize autonomy and circular organization of living systems (Maturana, 1975). The central characteristic of autopoietic systems is their operational unity. Systems are structurally linked with the medium in which they exist. This means they are in an energetic exchange with their environment. Because of their operational unity, they are at the same time autonomous.

Maturana believes that systems of higher order are made up of autopoietic systems of lower order (organisms). The state of the honey bees is an example of a higher order. It has a circular organization that is built upon an autopoietic system, the bees. The bees, in turn, have a circular organization that is based on another autopoietic system, the cells. The concept of autopoiesis was originally developed to analyze organisms as living systems. Meanwhile there have been many attempts to transfer the theory of autopoietic systems to the analysis of social systems (Luhmann, 1995, 1998; Hejl, 1982; Zeleny, Cornet, and Stoner, 1990). In these it is assumed that social systems are autopoietic systems of higher order, whose elements also represent autopoietic systems. Such a theory is close to Maturana's original thoughts.

Furthermore, the actions or communications of an autopoietic system can be seen as being responsible for the upkeep of autopoiesis. With this type of argumentation, which is stated by Luhmann (1995), the scientific logic of terms is completely discarded. Social systems are, by definition, autopoietic systems. In social systems, decisions are the structural elements. Decisions act as fuel for growth in social systems. Building on a general theory of social systems, Luhmann further suggests that economic organizations be viewed as autopoietic systems (Luhmann, 1998). Economic organizations are historically mature systems and orient themselves through the possibility of continuing their self-reproduction. The development of economic organizations essentially depends on their own dynamic.

Following Luhmann's theory, social systems in general and economic organizations in particular count as autopoietic systems, since a system's internal decisions leave room for self-renewal and growth. Luhmann's more generalized argument must be refined. Innovations function as decisions that keep economic organizations alive and guarantee their autopoietic growth. Economic organizations are, by definition, not autopoietic systems. Economic reality shows that a majority of companies are barely capable of realizing autopoietic growth, since only a limited amount of organizational self-renewal can be utilized. Whether or not a company is an autopoietic system depends, as will be shown later, on the way in which innovations are created.

Basics of Growth Theory

Companies develop over the course of their growth into complex organizations, which, to a great extent, evade the steering mechanisms of the classical management theories (Kanter, 1982; Kikuzawa, 1996; de Geus, 1997). In times of rapid and far-reaching changes, organizational forms, which only have a small amount of adaptation potential and limited mechanisms for complexity coping, are latently endangered in their future growth. Companies may be legal entities, but they are disturbingly mortal. Like organisms, companies exist primarily for their own survival and improvement: to fulfill their potential and to become as great as they can be.

In Japan this context is referred to as *daikigyobyo*, the big-business syndrome. The big-business syndrome can be recognized by the following symptoms: highly centralized and inflated bureaucracy, shuffling problems between departments, and an increase in detailed approval processes to reach decisions (micro-management) (Tateisi, 1985). A large number of hierarchy levels leads to organizational overcomplexity. This results in disturbances in the informational flow and finally to a decrease in reaction capability and efficiency. The organization is overstructured, overcontrolled, and overmanaged.

This disease is being caused by the growth of Japanese firms into gigantic corporations, and it is the ironic result of their very success. The discovery of a cure is a vital priority for the industry. The symptoms of the disease appear at various levels of the corporate organization, from top management down to the rank and file. In fact, it seems that the bureaucracy, the educational system, and the Japanese society as a whole have become infected by this disease, falling into a trap created by success. This irony of success is a common result of economic growth and increasing scale in countries everywhere, but there are reasons for fearing that its effects will be particularly damaging in Japanese society. One reason for this is that Japanese industry has surged to the fore much faster than industry in other countries, making it more reluctant to criticize and reform the systems that have brought success. Another reason is the high value Japanese businesses place on the seniority system and long-term employment guarantees. In the corporate order thereby created, it is unusually difficult to implement reforms that make organizations more flexible and bring in fresh air.

The affected companies are slowly dying. De Geus (1997) reports a survey that predicts 12.5 years is the average life expectancy of any company. The average life expectancy of a multinational corporation—Fortune 500 or its equivalent—is between forty and fifty years, noting that a third of the 1970s Fortune 500 had disappeared by 1983. In addition, 50 percent of exports in the United States are created by firms with nineteen or fewer employees. Companies with 500 or more employees account for only 7 percent of U.S. exports, and Fortune 500 companies account for only 10 percent of the U.S. economy, down from 20 percent in 1970. Such endemic failure is attributed to the focus of managers on profits and the bottom line rather than the viability of the organization. Contrary to popular opinion, Naisbitt (1994) argues that large companies must break up and become federations of small, autonomous, entrepreneurial companies if they are to survive.

An organizational form, generally referred to as *bunshaka*, is supposed to work against the cause of *daikigyobyo* and has achieved increased meaning in Japan. *Bunshaka* literally means "process (*ka*) of dividing (*bunkatsu*) into companies (*kaisha*)." In English *bunshaka* is translated as spin-off or devolution (Odagiri, 1992). The term devolution means that an occurred evolution is reversed or limited. The companies form subsidiary companies and transfer into these expelled functional and production areas. With this, a shrinking process is purposely carried out to reach an easily comprehensible and steerable organizational unit. The process of *bunshaka* is illustrated in Figure 3.4.

The functional areas I, II, III and IV of company A are taken out of the main company and develop into the central activities of subsidiary companies. In doing so, *bunshaka* occurs in several steps: first a change in the legal basic requirements occurs. Some departments or business areas are transformed into legal, self-reliant organizational units in which the employees are usually taken over and 100 percent of the capital shares are held by the main company.

If the subsidiary company achieves further growth after successful separation, it will employ co-workers to proactively resist a growth spurt. Furthermore, third parties can be invited to take over stocks, so that the financial basis is broadened. This process can continue until the employees originally taken over by the parent company are a minority and the share of the parent company is decreased to less than half. It can even happen that subsidiary companies reach total autonomy from the parent company or even try to dominate them.

FIGURE 3.4. Autopoietic and Allopoietic Growth

bunshaka

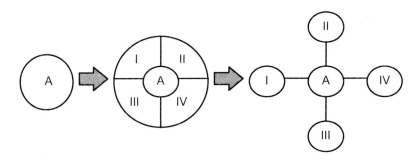

merger / acquisition

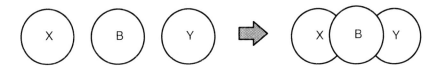

Fuji photo film, the world's largest film producer next to Kodak, was once a relatively insignificant subsidiary firm of a celluloid manufacturer, which in turn was the subsidiary of a trading firm. Today Fuji photo film dominates its original parent company. Another example is Toyota Motors, which was split off from Toyota Automatic Loom in 1937, and developed into a self-reliant and extremely successful firm in the following years. Toyota Automatic Loom still holds a 4.3 percent share in Toyota, but is now only the third largest shareholder. Toyota, which has a turnover twenty times larger than that of the original parent company, has a 25 percent share in Toyota Automatic Loom. Hitachi, today one of the largest electronics firms in the world, emerged in 1908 as a repair shop of Hitachi Mining, a traditional mining company.

A different growth strategy is found in Western companies. They often drive their growth forward by acquiring smaller companies or by merging with competitors (Kanter, 1982). New organizational units less often originate through internal self-reproduction in a company, but are more often taken into an existing structure from the outside. According to Figure 3.4, company B acquires companies X and Y and has thus strengthened its competitive position since it can take over competencies of these other companies and utilize them. However a latent danger exists that the internal structures could turn out to be unwieldy and confusing, since foreign organizational units must be integrated. Synergistic effects that should be reached with merger and acquisitions (M&A) activities often do not occur. The merged companies stay foreign bodies in a previously intact organization and block resources that could be used for other jobs.

The management of the overlapping areas between the different company parts can turn into a corporate task of highest priority. Matching different organizational cultures usually leads to internal heterogeneity and motivates the employees to optimize their own area at the disadvantage of the entire company. Visions of integrated technology companies, as they were promoted by Western companies in the 1980s, turned out to be a farce more often than not. M&A activities are usually avoided by Japanese companies, since the acquisition of one's own company by a competitor is usually seen as a humiliation by the employees (Kester, 1991). Consequently the Japanese refer to acquisition as *nottori* and *miuri,* which literally means "kidnapping" and "prostitution."

Bunshaka points out parallels to biological processes. The development of a company cannot be directly equated to the ontogenesis of an organism or to the development of a species in the evolutionary process. In the ontogenesis of a multicellular organism, functionally different cells develop, whereby this type of differentiation is already genetically preprogrammed. This contradicts the view of a company that can adapt to the market through individual innovations. A biological species furthermore modifies itself by having the offspring generation differ slightly from the parent generation. In the case of corporate evolution, the subsidiary companies can in contrast bring out totally new developmental models. Perhaps the most important difference between biological evolution and the growth of companies is that companies can actively and purposely influence the future, whereas in the case of biological evolutionary coincidence, genetic mutation plays a dominating role in the creation of innovations.

From a more abstract point of view, clear analogies between biological and organizational evolution become visible. The processes that take place during the development of a species correspond to the finding of solutions to cope with complexity (Calenbuhr, 1996). During the course of biological evolution, new and more complex species develop that are better adapted to the environment. Evolution can thus be seen as a process of optimization. This situation is reminiscent of how companies behave on the market and present new products, or rather how they change internally to secure their competitive ability and thus stay alive.

Corporate growth in the form of *bunshaka* is an autopoietic process. Autopoiesis turns living beings (companies) into autonomic organisms (organizational units). Autonomic organizational units derive their components through the operations that define their components. This provides a dynamic of never-ceasing structures. An autopoietic system can thus be genuinely described by its self-reproduction and self-renewal. *Bunshaka* is an autopoietic growth process, since companies do not continue their growth forever, but instead renew and reproduce their internal structures. The renewal shows in the relocation of functional areas into legal self-reliant organizational units and in the signing of cooperative agreements.

In contrast to *bunshaka*, the growth strategy of Western companies is a process that is referred to by Maturana as allopoietic (Maturana, 1975). Allopoietic systems do not grow through self-production of their components, but are constructed for certain reasons. As in artificial systems, bought-up companies are completely built into an existing organization. Usually they remain isolated from one another in the long run.

Growth Engine Innovations

Innovations are generally regarded as motivating forces of growth, since innovations offer companies the chance to differentiate themselves through superior offers and thus improve their competitive position (Robinson, 1988). The success of innovations calls upon competitors who try to imitate successful products. The products of the innovative company can now perhaps only be sold at decreasing prices. The company is forced to bring out further innovations. If it is no longer in the position to do so, it can lose its ability to compete medium-term. With this as the background, the ability to continuously produce innovations becomes a significant competitive factor. Success-oriented companies do not fight this change, but actively shape it.

In the post-World War II years, companies such as Pan Am, Rover, and AEG were seen as guaranteeing economic growth, because they launched innovations that were unique and directional in their industry. Today these companies have either totally vanished or were acquired by their competitors. The economic failure of these companies was not due to poor innovations. The problem was that too much time was needed to push through these innovations. In Europe and the United States, more radical product innovations are generally favored. Only after phases of extended basic research are the products placed on the market. The effort necessary for the success is not only large, but the outcome is unknown. They also often require greater and newer demands on the management competency (Drucker, 1988; Nonaka and Takeuchi, 1995).

In Japanese companies, the development of products linked to revolutionary new ideas is more the exception than the rule. Existing knowledge becomes the basis for building and from which new knowledge can be extracted and developed. Innovations aim less at the products that are finally brought onto the market, but more on the processes that lead to the products. The idea of competencies holds a special meaning in Japanese companies. With the strategy of incremental process innovations, Japanese companies are in a position to bring their products more quickly onto the desired market than their Western competitors. The innovative efforts are geared toward the customers' needs, whereby the development of new products is regarded as a continuous improvement process (Kagono et al., 1985). Figure 3.5 clarifies the Japanese and Western innovation strategies.

A classification of different innovation strategies can only generally exhibit the practice of Western and Japanese companies. It is always problematic to systemize strategies in an international comparison. Companies can be cited that will disprove these classifications. Sony's Walkman reminds us of an example of radical product innovation following a Western pattern. In regard to its culture and

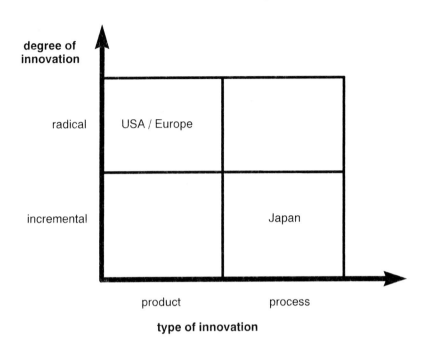

FIGURE 3.5. Innovations in Strategic Networks

growth structure, Sony, as Cusumano (1991) and Chikudate (1996) emphasize, is a firm more characterized by Western corporate culture and thus does not represent the majority of Japanese industries.

Incremental process innovations show interesting parallels to biology. During the course of evolution, larger advances such as the development of new organisms are never brought about in a single step. Changes in the genetic make-up, mutations, only lead to small changes on the level of internal processes that take place in an organism. The changes on the biochemical level can also lead to macroscopic changes during the course of evolution, such as new behavior, greater efficiency, etc. Biology thus only attempts relatively small innovations. Larger steps would most likely have a negative effect or even lead to death of the organism.

In this respect, the incremental changing processes of Japanese companies are in certain ways related to the biological way of evolution. Companies produce a steady outflow of innovations. The employees try to improve or refine existing processes. Incremental innovations may only lead to company growth in small steps, but they decrease the danger of halting or shrinking growth, which latently exists in risky, radical innovation steps. An important innovation goal is to create the basis for the realization of a diversification strategy. The activities of a company are defined by the components of the products and are thus widened by continuous innovation pushes. Innovations are not subordinate to the economic goals, but act as catalysts and activators for the company.

If innovations have piled up in a certain business, the decision can be made to release that division into autonomy as *bunshaka* or to keep it in the company as a central area. Autopoietically led economic organizations link an incremental innovation strategy to a decentralization strategy as found in the integration into strategic networks.

With the strategy of radical innovations, phases of growth alternate with phases of standstill. A long time goes by until a radical innovation has developed into a marketable product, so that the self-renewal energies of the company can become paralyzed. If complex products represent the goal of innovation strategies, and one does not assume that existing products can continuously be improved, then technological quantum leaps must inevitably be performed. By doing without continuous improvements, synergy effects that could lead to diversification in new technology fields are lost. The companies are forced to acquire other companies and to grow through organizational concentration in order to negate this disadvantage.

If a company does not quickly respond to market changes, it can easily become the victim of a takeover by a more powerful company. Companies that lie beyond the critical size and exert relative power can be so overloaded by bureaucracy that incremental innovations can only be achieved with great difficulty. In this case, other companies have to be bought up to close the innovation gaps in their own organization. Allopoietically led organizations combine a radical innovation strategy with an organizational concentration strategy.

Case Example: Hitachi

The electronics firm, Hitachi, developed as a repair shop at the beginning of the century from the mining firm Hitachi Mining through *bunshaka*. The mining firm with headquarters in Hitachi, a city north of Tokyo, is today many times surpassed in its importance. With the founding of the firm as a spin-off from an existing company, Hitachi is an example of an autopoietic growth process.

Hitachi rarely made acquisitions in the following years and grew goal oriented through autopoietic self-renewal and clever cooperation politics. The first phase of *bunshaka* started in 1956. Three important functional areas were converted into self-reliant subsidiaries. Hitachi Metal, Hitachi Denshi, and Hitachi Construction Machinery developed. Up to the present, 200 subsidiaries followed in this fashion. The subsidiaries (*kogaisha*) for their part create new subsidiaries that are referred to as "grandchild firms" (*magosha*). There are over 600 *magosha*, and Hitachi usually does not interfere with their business and guidelines. This task is done by the *kogaisha*. Over time an organizational family tree has crystallized (see Figure 3.6).

By growing along an organizational tree, Hitachi has kept an easily comprehensible size. With approximately 80,000 employees worldwide, Hitachi employs approximately one-third of the employees that would be necessary for Western competitors such as

FIGURE 3.6. Organizational Tree of Hitachi

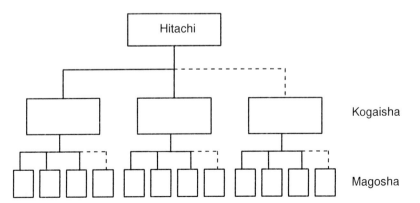

Siemens or General Electric to achieve a turnover of comparable size. Up until the end of the 1980s, while Siemens and General Electric were still diversifying into different technology areas by buying up firms, Hitachi went the opposite way and developed through internal growth, combined with the integration into strategic networks. Today Hitachi is marked by an extremely lean and well-organized organizational structure.

Battered by a global downturn in the semiconductor market, the company currently expects a decline in sales. This prompted the integrated electronics and electric machinery maker to announce a far-reaching restructuring plan designed to turn its business around. Hitachi plans to reorganize its consumer-products manufacturing units into separate entities via *bunshaka* and to further streamline the division.

Two types of organizational units can be distinguished that can be released as *bunshaka* into an autonomy of a self-reliant subsidiary. One is venture units that are created in the parent company with the goal to venture into new fields of technology. As soon as the venture units have their first successes, they are displaced into self-reliant subsidiaries. The employees working in the venture units are specialists who are distinguished through special qualifications or abilities.

Furthermore, firm areas that are no longer part of the center activities of Hitachi or that only have limited competitive abilities are taken out of the firm. The best example of this is the area of consumer electronics, which was displaced to a *kogaisha*. For the semiconductor production, a subsidiary was also created in which products that are in the developing stage of the production cycle are manufactured. New generations of semiconductors, however, are being developed in central research labs of the parent firm and produced in their headquarters. Qualification and achievement levels of the employees of the subsidiaries often lie below the usual standard of the parent firm. Such a personnel transfer is termed *shukko,* and is especially useful to forgo dismissals and to still give the employees career perspectives.

A contradictory picture appears which shows that departments with employees who are especially innovative and strong achievers as well as departments with employees who are average or achieve less than average are taken into subsidiaries in the form of *bunsha-ka*. Central activities, however, remain in the parent firm. When a subsidiary gets into financial trouble or has to fight structural problems, it is supported by the parent firm as well as by other subsidiaries. It is remarkable that firms of the Hitachi group do not necessarily get components and building parts from other firms in the group. If quality and price of a competing firm are better, the transaction occurs there. The firms are relatively autonomous in their decisional competencies.

In most cases, product developments occur simultaneously in the parent firm as well as in one or more subsidiaries, in order to give different concepts a chance. Redundancies are consciously accepted. Synergistic effects between the firms occur since active information politics are pursued across the entire firm network. Employees of the subsidiaries are also invited to Hitachi's training classes. If the parent firm and subsidiary manufacture similar products in one area, the employees regularly meet to exchange their experiences. Incremental innovation processes are purposely driven forward by supporting teamwork, quality assurance meetings, and total quality control management.

A fine balance exists between competition and cooperation within the Hitachi group of companies. Independence of each entity is encouraged by the rule that any group company ought not to have huge portions of its business with other group companies. Although they are not true entrepreneurs, the executive managers who are appointed to run a new spin-off are given almost total autonomy in recruiting their own workers and seeking new customers. Moreover, group companies in the same line of business compete with each other in obtaining orders from the same customers. Despite such competition, the cohesion of the group is maintained because managers in different companies may have once worked together in the same company.

SYMBIOSIS

The logic behind the most economically useful manufacturing method is universal. It works in Japan as well as in the West, but it works because of adaptation to the competition and less because a switch between contracting companies can occur at liberty if their products are cheaper. The adaptation of price and quality is preferably based on existing relationships and changed according to prior agreements. Put differently, the logic of economic obligation is realized within the logic of lasting human relations, but not by sacrificing human relationships to meet economic obligations.

The subordination of economic logic to the importance of human relations gives Japan its own physiognomy. Japanese companies do not exist as cellular units but as a symbiotic society that is linked in nets of relationships that are complex and appear impermeable from the outside. The relationship between companies bound to one another in strategic networks is looser than the one that organizational members within a company have. Yet it is still close enough to make a network into a relatively stable unit, held together by a sort of reciprocal security and insurance. Purchasing stock from one another, transferring of technical knowledge, and generally voting on market strategy questions gives an almost unshatterable basis of trust—a symbiotic relationship based on mutuality.

Symbiosis is a universal concept that is particularly used in a biological environment of animals and plants. Symbiotic living beings in nature supplement each other's abilities by letting others share in their individual evolutionary advantages. Many organisms regularly live together whereby both partners profit from this arrangement. The "nationalized" organisms belong to various groups. Symbiotic relationships occur between bacteria and unicellular organisms, between algae, between animals and higher plants, and between animals. Even the relationship of dependency is very different in the various symbioses.

Symbiosis of animals and plants is useful for the nutrition of one partner and for the reproduction of the other partner. One of the most remarkable examples is the symbiosis of petal plants and pollinating animals. A luring medium, developed by the plant during the course of history, is the nectar-producing gland and pollen for insects. The petal structure is adapted to the insect's shape in such a way that the dispensing of nectar and pollen serves the transfer of a part of the pollen to the next petal. The interaction between insect and plant in such a close physical relationship proves to be beneficial to both.

The symbiosis between two organisms requires the altruistic behavior of all involved. Altruism can be analyzed in various ways. Pure or strict altruism is an unanswered sacrifice for the sake of other organisms. A more complex view is weak altruism, which basically means open self-interest. Weak altruism means that an organism, for a short time, sacrifices its optimum adaptation but in the long run receives more than it gave. In case we want to accuse a symbiont of rational behavior, this definition might lead us directly to a theory that deals with questions about cooperatives from a strategic point of view, the game theory.

Basics of the Game Theory

The game theory shows that the cooperation of players leads to a better outcome than if every player acted independently. Unlike the systems theory and the growth theory, the game theory focuses on the return of the cooperation. Since Von Neumann's and Morgenstern's classic *Theory of Games and Economic Behavior* (Neumann and Morgenstern, 1944) the game theory has been applied many times in the analysis of economic systems (Axelrod, 1984; Aoki, 1984; Tirole, 1988; Nielson, 1988; Cameren, 1991). Interactions between companies in an economic setting that is characterized by uncertainty and incomplete information can be seen as a game with zero outcome, or as positive sum outcome or negative sum outcome. In a zero sum game, one company wins, while the others lose. In a positive sum game, all companies can improve their shares, while in a negative sum game, every company loses.

For a description of the theoretical background of economic behavioral strategies, one can refer to the standard works by Axelrod (1984) and Aoki (1984). Axelrod discusses the central question, under which circumstances does cooperative behavior occur in a world without central direction and supported by egotism? In the development of his ideas he assumes the game's standard situation, as in the famous Prisoner's Dilemma game, and bases them on the following matrix: The mutual gain of two players is maximized if both cooperate and is lowest if both do not cooperate. Every player can maximize his or her gain if the partner cooperates. Axelrod bases his thoughts on the Prisoner's Dilemma, a game that the participants play several times or in which they take several turns.

Axelrod demonstrates that if generalized competition is a requisite, cooperatives develop in the medium run because cooperation offers selection advantages to the players. Particularly if a mutual goal is to be achieved, individuals who have not had much sympathy for one another begin to work together. The principle tit for tat, as you do to me, I do to you, is collectively stable, and can only be tackled mutually once the future starts throwing warning shadows. Tit for tat behavior of a partner only leads to stable, cooperative behavior if the other partner also responds with this behavior or constantly cooperates. If all partners use the tit for tat strategy, a collective stability can develop. This concept is shown in Figure 3.7.

In a transitional phase in which collective stability can set in, the players change from competitive to cooperative behavior. It is evident that in this case, elements of competition cannot be totally given up or negated. The players are not strict but rather weak altruists. Although there is theoretically no best strategy to secure

FIGURE 3.7. Tit for Tat

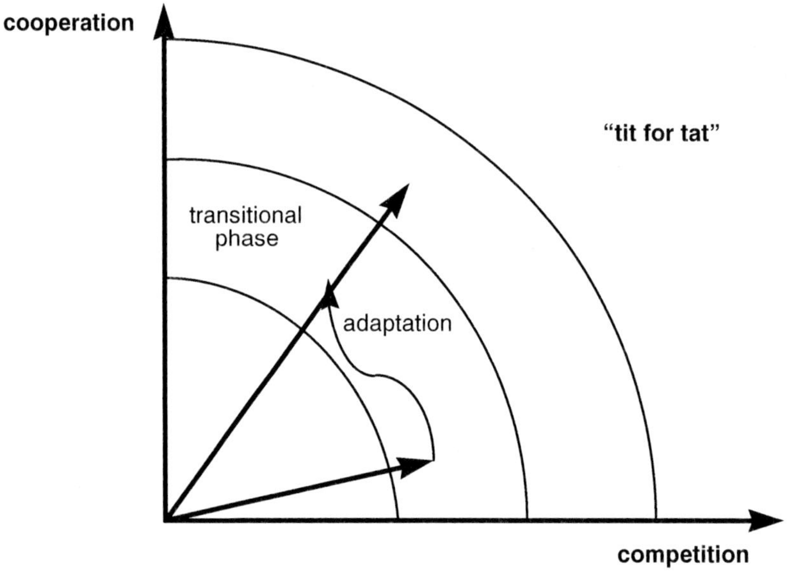

cooperative behavior, since the behavior of a partner cannot be predicted with certainty, many things point to the tit for tat strategy as supporting cooperative behavior of the partners through its learning features. One sets a good example and cooperates. By directly retaliating the noncooperative behavior of the partner, one discourages him or her from cooperation. Because of a willingness to forgive past noncooperative behavior of the partner under the condition of future cooperation, one encourages cooperation.

This is valid not only for individuals, who can decide to cooperate because they see problems ahead, but mutatis mutandis also for economic organizations that try to secure their ability to compete through the strategy of a network cooperative. In this sense Aoki (1984) projected the general game theory onto the institutionalized firm theory. He assumes that the ability of a company to compete is determined by its network-specific knowledge potential or a so-called *organizational income*. Companies maximize their organizational income, which means the objective use in the form of competition advantages, if they compete with other organizations. The organizational income is evenly distributed among the cooperating companies in ratios equal to their previous work. The distribution occurs for the long term and reaches a balance at a value that is mutually found to be fair. This means for a short period of time individual shares of the organizational income are not necessarily balanced.

If a company acting in a cooperative network does not consciously cooperate, it can then only maximize its organizational income if the other partners continue to cooperate. A noncooperation is equivalent to the dissolving or instability of a network, since all other companies linked in the network are worse off than with a cooperative dissolution. If cooperatives are perceived in the sense of a zero sum game, then losers will always be found next to the winners. The basic idea of maximizing benefits lies in the specific influencing of the partner's behavior with one's own cooperative behavior.

In continuing Axelrod's and Aoki's ideas, the negative sum game can be banned from the practice of network management, since cooperative agreements usually arise from the intention to open up new fields of actions, not gamble them away. If all participating parties lose more through cooperation than they win, then a cooperative becomes obsolete. This does not mean that negative sum games do not exist in the economic reality. Through the contracting of a cooperative, the participating partners can block each other, since possible developmental trajectories remain opportunistically closed. In such cases cooperatives are usually dissolved early on. From an analytic point of view, this case therefore has no relevance.

The game situation of companies in a cooperating network association requires that the actions of companies, similar to those of individuals, are linked in a cause-reaction chain. In a network between companies, such a rational selectivity is only partially existent. The interactions of companies are almost never totally bilateral, but are recursively branched together in a network of complex exchange relationships. The game theory reduces the economic reality to a pair of players, by either aggregating actions of several players to two players or by forgoing their potential embedding into the network structure. The actions of the companies of a market segment are directly or indirectly related to one another and thus influence the game situation of a multitude of companies. The classic game theory also assumes that every player knows his or her own benefit and that of his or her partner (Nielson, 1988). This assumption also can be weakened since the interactions between companies do not necessarily have to exist in a linear and rational way. The players operate with an incomplete perception of their environment. They are not necessarily capable of determining the optimal strategy in light of their beneficial function and of anticipating rational choices of their opponents.

Since the interactive cooperation actions obviously do not satisfy the linear developmental sequence of the game theory, we shall leave the classic game theory and talk about *circular game situations*. In circular game situations there are no direct and rational adaptations to the actions of the partner companies. Instead, the game situations emerge from the partners' interactions, so that they are regarded as the results of exchange actions and not as their requirements. Circular game situations widen the action reality from archetypical two-player/two-strategy games to a network of interacting players with a multitude of strategic options for each.

Weak Altruism

Companies that combine vertical and horizontal learning processes and whose actions in the context of circular game situations can thus lead to a positive sum game probably have the best chances to secure their competitive abilities in the long run. They combine an organizationally caused orientation to the interior with an orientation to the exterior aimed at a network association. Symbiotic network management leans on the development of innovations, competencies, and cultures and is thus an integral beginning for organizational self-renewal.

Companies require learning steps of all three learning orders: deductive and adaptive learning for continuous product and process innovations, generative and stimulative learning for the extension of competencies, and evolutive and stimulative learning for the development of culturally progressive organizational models. The important task is to find the right mix of learning sequences and not to neglect a few aspects of knowledge management.

Since the early 1990s, the Japanese have come to the conclusion that many companies seem to have a good learning mix and thus could increase their companies' growth, but that the learning success occurs at the expense of the cooperative partners. Japanese companies carried out horizontal learning processes without having their partner companies participate in their knowledge in the same manner (Hamel, 1991). According to Teramoto, Richter, and Iwasaki (1993) and Teramoto (1993), companies being led according to the principles of a pluralistic network culture fare much better in comparison to a conservatively led company.

With this realization a new creed developed in Japan, stating that a company's environment should be used to learn, but also knowledge should be given to the company's environment. This corporate philosophy is referred to as *kyosei,* and means symbiotic interaction with the surrounding companies (Murakami, 1992). Akio Morita, former chairman of Sony, propagated and lived by the idea of a symbiotic interaction (Morita, 1992). He advocates a stronger and qualitatively more balanced partnership between Japanese and Western companies. Partnership should not be a one-way street, but a long-term relationship supported by mutual trust.

Through efforts to elevate productivity, slash costs, and improve quality, Japan's companies have managed to manufacture internationally competitive products that have made broad inroads into many overseas markets. To say that a product is competitive is basically to say that it attracts consumers. By turning out just such products, Japan's companies have benefited consumers throughout the world. When adopting the perspective of producers, however, a different picture emerges, since the success of Japan's products has come at a cost to competitors in other countries, leading to economic friction. Friction is an inevitable fact of life for economies and companies, but when firms from different cultures clash and compete, the opportunity for various types of problems increases. If these problems are to be minimized, it is essential that competition take place in accordance with the rules accepted by all the players involved. Now that Japan's businesses have grown so large, they must pay particularly close attention to the need for playing by international rules.

Japan's firms need to develop a stronger awareness of their responsibilities and roles in society at home and abroad. Because they acquired great influence over the communities in which they operate, they are being asked to become good corporate citizens. In recent years they have been making rapid progress on this front. Awareness of the needs has spread from the top management on down, and *kyosei* programs are being conducted to strengthen the ties between the company and the community.

It is important to note that *kyosei* is not conducted out of pure altruism or charity. The self-interest in Japan lies in *hateke zukuri* (ploughing the field) for future eventuality. One never knows when one will have to become indebted to others (*osewa ni naru*).

Growth of a system that is not linked to an environment with similar growth can, as Senge (1990) shows, stagnate or even decline. Limitations arise if a shortage of resources occurs or if the system's environment, due to closeness of the optimum, no longer permits expansive growth. Similarly Christensen (1991), Clark (1991), Pearce and Warford (1993), and Group of Lisbon (1995) share the opinion that growth always should be seen as sustainable. The consequences of the actions should not question the evolutionary potential of the environment. Zeleny (1996) demands a free trade-off interaction between actor and environment.

According to the *kyosei* vision, learning processes can also be supported and activated in their organizational environment. *Kyosei* aims for the coevolution of the cooperating companies. Figure 3.8 illustrates a learning model that advocates a profit for all participating companies.

Next to vertical learning processes, horizontal ones occur simultaneously. Companies voluntarily render their innovations, competencies, and culturally formed behavioral patterns to balance out the development and power potential in the cooperative network. In doing so, the growth of one company is linked to that of the surrounding network. In this sense the long-term strategies include the interests of other companies.

Symbiotic interaction does not mean that a company's internal goals are abandoned for the sake of cooperative goals. The principle of altruism that is based on the sacrifice of developmental potentials

FIGURE 3.8. Symbiotic Interaction

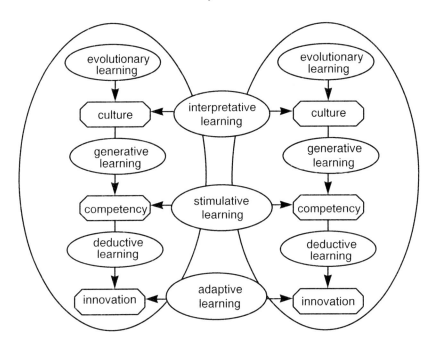

for the good of others is not valid in its strict form. However, one principle that Simon defined as weak altruism achieves importance (Simon, 1983). Companies initially sacrifice developmental potential in order to indirectly receive knowledge in the long run, which will overcompensate for the initial sacrifice. With weak altruism, the conscious expectation that one might later need the person whom one is helping now and that he or she might then also be altruistic and cooperative, plays an important role. It is questionable indeed whether altruism even exists in its pure form. Pure altruism without hope for mutuality is one of the rarest behavioral forms in nature.

In contrast to egotism, altruism aims for the integration of the individual or organization into a living environment. The starting point for the observation of altruistic behavior is the fact that individual organisms are social, which means they live in groups. Groups provide protection and encourage organizational learning. The joining of individuals to groups must have obviously been beneficial during evolution. Thus, there is almost no completely solitary living organism in nature. Even loners must come into social interaction for the sake of reproduction. Group life of individuals automatically includes altruistic behavior. A group of pure egotists would be a contradiction.

The advantages of altruistic behavior appear both on the level of individuals and on the group level. With cooperation the survival of the individuals is more likely than if everyone competes against one another, because the group stays intact. Social societies in Asia are essentially founded on this central idea. So-called *relationship accounts* are widely spread: if a task is performed for someone, in the sense of altruism, then this task is kept as a credit in an imaginary account. Balanced relationship accounts are sought, in which first of all, explicitly made promises or future relationships are found. Second, purposely sought dependency relationships are reflected.

Case Example: Mitsubishi Kagaku

Japanese companies in the chemical industry have in the past predominantly invested in products that were needed for further technological advances in the automobile and electronics industry. This is why Japanese companies hold a top position in the areas of new materials while there is still a technological gap in the area of bulk chemicals in comparison to Western firms such as DuPont, Bayer, or Imperial Chemical Industries (ICI) (Itami, 1991b). In the past, one way to increase their ability to compete in the world market was to enter into strategic alliances with Western firms.

One characteristic of the Japanese chemical industry is that their companies are generally smaller than their European or American counterparts. The largest Japanese manufacturers are placed in the middle of the worldwide ranking. The Japanese MITI has tried in the past to support the chemical industry by giving government assistance. These politics encouraged many companies that were foreign to the chemical industry to expand into this industry. Due to continuous government assistance, a negative selection of weak competitors could not take place.

The current picture of the Japanese chemical industry shows a multitude of companies that barely distinguish themselves from one another in size and production areas. Until recently, companies with a national leadership position could not be found. In the early 1990s, a national champion emerged that climbed into the group of international leading chemical companies by using the symbiotic effect of internal interactions. It was created by the cooperation of two firms of the Mitsubishi-*keiretsu*, when Mitsubishi Kasei and Mitsubishi Sekiyu combined to form Mitsubishi Kagaku. Learning processes occur in the firm on a vertical as well as horizontal level. Mitsubishi Kagaku entered into more than twenty cooperatives with Western partners in order to learn their technologies, competencies, and culturally shaped organizational models. The horizontal learning processes were complemented with vertical learning processes as illustrated in Figure 3.9.

Mitsubishi Kagaku concentrated in the past on abilities that increased leeway in the development of products and processes. The firm tried to create competencies in the fields of new materials and special chemicals in order to achieve major products such as film, resin, and ceramics for the electronics, automobile, and printing industries. The major products were used in the final products such as insulation materials for automobile brakes. Resin is used for the manufacturing of drugs, semiconductors, and food industry products. Mitsubishi Kagaku's success is based on the diversification sur-

FIGURE 3.9. Cooperation Strategies of Mitsubishi Kagaku

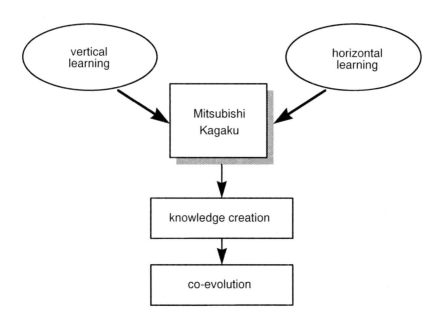

rounding major products. This significantly increases the basis for problem solving. The employees are asked to develop market-driven products and to share their individual knowledge with colleagues during the developmental process in order to increase the company's expertise. Deductive learning is consistently taught and practiced, thus helping the company to continuously create new products.

Mitsubishi Kagaku was further able to develop competencies through generative learning. The company is experimenting with a new form of organizational structure, which supports working in project groups. Such project groups are miniature companies that act autonomously and can direct themselves. Existing business units are being transferred into the smallest possible units and hierarchies are abandoned. The distribution of skills between different project groups leads to advantages in differentiation and cost. This structure makes self-organization by the members of a project group possible, so that a stronger process of knowledge generation in the company can be introduced. At first glance, Mitsubishi Kagaku seems to be an unstructured conglomerate of miniature business units. But the miniature organizational units allow the employees' ideas to span several manufacturing areas. This promotes the opening up of competencies in the entire company, which starts to become more homogenous in its entirety. The open and flexible manner in which the company is managed allows the building and nursing of competencies that, once generated, can be transferred into new products or processes.

Forms of evolutive learning are actively being utilized by deductive and generative learning. Mitsubishi Kagaku is an example that evolutive learning can lead to a paradigmatic change of the company's culture through strengthening competencies as well as products and processes. The market shares stagnated in the late 1980s and new industry fields could only be opened with great difficulty. After a phase of intensive evolutive learning at the beginning of the 1990s, Mitsubishi Kagaku experienced growth that catapulted the firm to the leading spot of the Japanese chemical industry. Up until this time the firm was regarded as bureaucratic and slow. The employees lacked the motivation to work toward achieving the repositioning of the firm. After a change in the top management, Mitsubishi Kagaku gave a project team the task of changing the organizational culture and thus the learning behavior of the employees. The goal was to pull the employees out of the dried-up organizational structure and to motivate them for competency development. A change in dynamic did indeed occur that helped position the firm as an innovative trendsetter. The employees unlearned their old rationality models. The campaign resulted in building competencies in the field of biotechnology and led to the introduction of a line of new materials. Thus, the cultural change was noticeable even in the products.

The described learning processes are supplemented by horizontal learning processes. Mitsubishi Kagaku has special abilities to accumulate knowledge through interfirm cooperative agreements. The company's focus in the past was on acquiring usable product technologies that made it possible to achieve similar innovations as the cooperative partners. In an alliance with the American chemical firm Monsanto, for example, Mitsubishi Kagaku was able to acquire products that it changed slightly. Through further improvements the company developed a slightly newer product that was superior to the original, and brought it into the market. Such adaptive learning processes made it possible for the firm to catch up to its cooperative partners and to increase its own basis of technology. When the alliance was dissolved in 1990, the Japanese firm received the largest share of joint venture activities. A new alliance was created containing only a few products; it is substantially smaller than the original cooperative. Mitsubishi Kagaku was able to successfully learn the skills of the partners so that the alliance became unnecessary.

At the end of the 1980s, Mitsubishi Kagaku began redefining the goal criteria for interfirm relationships. The goal was no longer to possess single technologies, but rather to build new competencies with the help of strategic networks. Competencies were developed in a line of technology tie-ups with innovative companies of the biotechnology industry. Within a relatively short time, biotechnology was defined as a new field of business and was built into a competency.

In recent years, Mitsubishi Kagaku has increasingly made cooperative agreements with Western partners to study and learn their culturally based organizational behavior. In this way, the company became allied with the German chemical giant Hoechst, to learn its R&D strategies and concepts and to use it as a role model for radical product innovations. Mitsubishi Kagaku had previously focused on incremental product innovations and aspired to strengthen its own skills basis. Both companies combined their resources in R&D, production, and sale of paints and were able to strengthen their competitive ability with this alliance. The alliance was a catalyst for new organizational behavior within the company, since it caused a change to a more European corporate culture.

With the beginning of the 1990s, network cooperations are no longer set up, managed, and developed for the exclusive sake of an individual advantage. Instead, knowledge is actively shared with the partners according to the *kyosei* vision. The *kyosei* vision as symbiotic action has been manifested in the corporation strategy and is used as a testing device for all alliances. Hoechst was able to profit from the company's symbiotic belief. It is due to this basic belief that Mitsubishi Kagaku has been able to have continuous growth over the last few years.

Chapter 4

Management of Strategic Networks

Companies act in a complex environment in which no company can be understood without the knowledge of its relationships to other companies. To compete means to position one's company in a network rather than to penetrate markets with aggressive strategies. The building and maintenance of relationships between companies becomes one of the most important tasks of managers (Eccles and Crane, 1987; Hakansson, 1989; Hakansson and Snehota, 1995; Richter and Teramoto, 1996; Chisholm, 1997; Gemünden, Ritter, and Heydebreck, 1996).

The management of strategic networks is often described in the literature as a transaction of products and services in the context of social communication between cooperative partners (Dwyer, Schurr, and Oh, 1987; Snow, Miles, and Coleman, 1992; Ford et al., 1998). According to this idea, strategic networks can be managed and cooperative relationships can be developed. Influential network managers arrange the network culture according to the idea that the economic reality is shapeable and plannable. This idea overlooks the fact that strategic networks are exposed to environmentally induced dynamics, for one, and the systems internal momentum for another. The multilayering and the latent instability in relationships between companies, as Gadde and Mattson (1987) remark, leaves the question to the planability and navigability and thus the entire management of strategic networks in general. Within the network an endogenous change of the existing power and influence structure can occur with a change in the basic interorganizational relationship. The relationships can go from the growth phase to the maturation phase. A single company finally can leave the network, and a new company, which initially does not meet the minimum requirements for a consistent structure, can enter the network. This has serious consequences for the management of networks that consequently must be recognized as unstable.

Engwall and Johanson (1990) go so far as to claim that strategic networks are marked by uncontrollability for the single network company as well as for a group of several network companies. The authors explain this finding with the fact that strategic networks are the result of transactions and interactions between interdependent, yet partially autonomous participants. The participants' autonomy is larger, the more fragmented the industry in which they act. This uncontrollability more or less calls for the *planned evolution* of networks.

The position of the planned evolution implies the task of imagining total controllability of the organizational—in this case, interorganizational, events, without having to completely do without the management of such (Van de Ven, Walker, and Liston, 1979; Van de Ven and Walker, 1984). Teramoto et al. (1993), who also advocate this, have generally found an absence of master plans in their studies of Japanese management strategies. If opportunities arise from the interaction with the company's environment that were not previously used, a change in course can be undertaken spontaneously and painlessly.

The term planned evolution is a hybrid in that it unites two opposing elements. Planning includes navigation and management; evolution includes spontaneity and self-organization. Planned evolution encompasses the influence of the economic environment and the admittance of self-organized processes. Due to linking, self-organized processes can be found in networklike organizational forms. Impulses sent out by network companies are being received by others. Changing processes, which are always connected to the existing structure and culture of the network, for example to traditions, are being supported, weakened, or even blocked. Due to the loose structure of the systems elements, the result is barely determinable or plannable. Although purposely stimulated, the result can never be completely navigated by the initiator.

The strategic network appears superficially stable, although this stability is built on the processes of continuous change (Morgan, 1986). Because of the permeable, autopoietic, and symbiotic nature of strategic networks, constant plans and their realization in the sense of complete action cycles are rarely possible. In the place of deterministic planning with follow-up actions, the mechanism of organizational learning sets in.

In the literature about decision-oriented management ideas, action cycles are usually characterized through a number of phases (Beckhard and Harris, 1978). Traditionally, an organization's ability to act is manifested through its ability to perform complete action cycles that contain all phases. If action cycles are not even initiated or if they are stopped after a few phases, then this indicates a lack of action ability. The phase theory for management processes in strategic networks apparently must be totally given up. The momentum that strategic networks show rarely permits a determination into planning phases. Instead, the management of strategic networks is based on continuous negotiation between the conditions of the cooperative partners through organizational learning. Globally viewed, the function of the managers in strategic networks consists of organizing those networks in the tension field of flexibility and legitimacy, and of mutually generating new knowledge with other companies, which will increase the ability to compete and thus increase the level of organizational evolution.

With this, network management implicates, as Uzzi (1997) demands, not only an increased acceptance of interdependencies, but also the definition of network boundaries. The management of strategic networks can span different parts of the value creation chain: manufacturer-consumer relationships in the just-in-time production (*logistics cooperation*), mutual research and development (*technology cooperation*) or the entrance to new markets (*globalization cooperation*). The management of strategic networks often refers to several parts of the value chain. Logistics courses, research and development, and globalization withdraw from deterministic management control, since the actions of other network companies are not plannable—merely influenceable. Network management thus runs along a planned evolution.

LOGISTICS COOPERATION

Logistics that are typical for Japan are manifested through just-in-time and *kanban* systems (Poirier and Reiter, 1996; Tokunaga,

Altmann, and Demes, 1992) and must be regarded under the basic conditions of the Japanese sales organization, in order to be fair to the historical and culture-specific determinants of the logistics cooperation in Japan. The quest for an efficient organization of the Japanese economy cannot be resolved by concentrating on just-in-time production, but should be evaluated in the sense of systematic rationalization. This involves an integrative process- and company-spanning rationalization strategy based on the intra- and interfirm linking of the entire value chain. Consequently, the relationship between supplier and buyer on the first step of the supplier pyramid is important, and succeeding parts of the supply chain are important as well. Thus the social-cultural relevancy becomes apparent and this can have an effect on necessary changes in working conditions of such a supply system.

After World War II, specific company structures were developed for Japan and pushed by the manufacturers. In doing so, the manufacturers' goal was not only to secure quality that would meet the standards of their products, but also to build a stable sales basis (Monden, 1991; Miyashita and Russel, 1994). The complexity of the sales system is significant, since the distribution of goods follows a multistep chain of companies. Japan has more than twice the number of large and small retailers as other industrial nations (Fruin, 1992). The chain begins with manufacturing, then to marketing companies, and from there to agencies, to large retailers or bulk buyers, and then to small retailers until the products finally reach the consumer. The manufacturers are often financially interwoven with the single steps of the sales chain, which gives the manufacturer great influence on the business. An oligopolitical structure of the large retailers is subdivided into many vertical steps and corresponds to a fragmented small retail structure.

The link of the manufacturer to the distribution chain requires close agreement in logistical questions, since the mere sale of the goods to the consumer by bringing in a logistical service company would be an autonomous market transaction and would not be in accordance with the complex Japanese net of distribution (Miyashita and Russel, 1994). Along with delivery security, reliability, and flexibility, the suppliers must also maintain continuous adaptability in addition to their obligation to uphold loyalty and quality during the supplying period. This includes keeping the production processes flexible and ensuring that production and supply plans meet the needs of the consumer.

With the increasing importance of production in systemically linked manufacturing associations, the demand to shape logistics between the companies also increases. Cooperative partners in vertical and horizontal exchange relationships supply one another with goods and services or exchange personnel for mutually pursued development projects. Macbeth (1996) concludes from this that organizational barriers within and between companies can cause enormous mistakes in logistic chains. The cooperative partners usually plan the area of influence on the logistics chain separately, so that in the worst case, although parts of the logistics chain are optimized, redundancies and unnecessary costs affect the operation.

An attempt to eliminate such mistakes can be found in optimizing the logistics chain. With the help of a problem structure analysis and formalizing, the reorganization of all relevant inner- and inter-company courses to achieve the corresponding logistics chain can be accomplished. By mediating between project groups, the important variables and restrictions of the logistics chain can be balanced and a solution suitable for each partner can be found.

Optimizing the Logistics Chain

The logistical production runs and the imminent system costs have developed into competitive factors. This is due to the close interlocking relationship between supplier and manufacturer in the different phases of the value chains. Supplying companies increasingly calculate their production for synchronized delivery and utilization time in order to achieve advantages in time and cost over their competitors. The inner-company optimization of logistics usually works quite well, but the coordination between the supplier and manufacturer is often extremely critical (Christopher, 1993; Poirier and Reiter, 1996). The optimization of the logistics chain usually ends with transporting the products from the supplier to the manufacturer. A coordination between supplier and manufacturer usually fails due to the inability to synchronize production as well as discrepancies between the demanded and actual delivery. Also difficult to coordinate are the need to reduce storage time as well as problems in passing on costs from the manufacturer to the supplier.

Optimizing the logistical sequence in the supplier company requires viewing the entire logistics chain. This includes knowing the storage site and capacity of the intermediate storage sites for raw materials, knowing the transport mechanisms, and the distribution of goods and further activities with the manufacturing company. The creation of the logistics chain should include processes with the supplier as well as with the customer, since optimizing within a company alone usually only leads to partial optimization. The activities of the value chain should be closely linked to the needs of the market, so that goods can be distributed at the right time, to the right place, in the right amounts, and with the right quality.

The study and optimizing of the entire logistics chain is based on the idea that companies ideally have permeable organizational boundaries. Such a company interacts with cooperative partners in a strategic network. Companies therefore develop together with other competing companies by mutual utilization of expertise through logistical processes. Supplier and manufacturer inform each other about their logistical processes and thus optimize their entire production processes. Figure 4.1 shows this connection.

Forrester (1958) developed a theory at the end of the 1950s that he called *supply-chain management*. The idea states that the function's purchasing, manufacturing, storage, and distribution should be planned and navigated as a unit. The goal is to decrease the stock and to optimally use capacities as well as to guarantee loyalty in supplying customers. With this, the focus of the logistic is shifted from stock optimization to process optimization.

This shift of emphasis is the requisite for an effective and efficient layout to perform all necessary processes for the customer. Supply-chain management implies that the single cost elements are optimized along a chain of logistics in the sense of *systems costs*. The term systems cost groups all relevant costs that are to be determined as part of a logistics plan. Whoever wants to take responsibility for the entire flow of materials and goods will probably not primarily look at isolated cost savings in single stations of the logistics chain, but rather at the sum of all costs over the entire chain. The goal of the integral logistics plan is to decrease system costs with sufficient willingness to supply.

FIGURE 4.1. Holistic Planning of the Logistics Chain

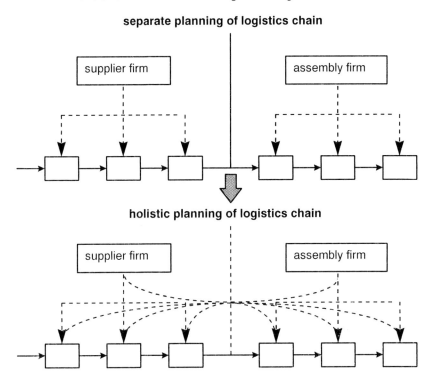

The task of creating an integral logistic system between supplier and manufacturer often bears conflicts that can only be solved by considering the basic rules of both companies. Thus, aspects other than pure calculated costs, company political aspects, questions about worker participation, all the way up to social aspects must be included. Furthermore, the reevaluation of all relevant costs becomes necessary.

A new breed of companies commands factories and supply networks around the world. Increasingly, they also manage their customers' entire product lines, offering an array of services from design to inventory management to delivery and after-sales service. "Outsourcing," a practice that has been around for decades, does not begin to describe the phenomenon. In place of traditional contracting relationships between client and supplier, arrangements with so-called "supercontractors" represent a sort of extended enterprise—a set of partnerships between product developers and specialists in components, distribution, retailing, and manufacturing.

The resulting organization can behave like a single, closely knit corporation—only better. Its strategies can slash time and costs from the supply chain, the process between the invention of a new product and the time it reaches the customer.

The effect on innovation could be huge. Spinning off manufacturing and other noncore functions allows big firms to focus new investments where they get the most bang: on research and marketing. Because the strategy reduces the need for capital and in-house operations expertise, startups face far lower barriers in bringing new technologies to the market.

Uniform Logistics Concepts

Long production runs become noticeable in high binding of capital assets. Although the production sites of two companies linked in a network geographically often lie close to each other, product storage usually occurs with the supplier as well as with the manufacturer. Due to the autonomy of partial processes of the logistics chain, a high handling expenditure manifests itself in frequent repackaging and transport processes. Consequently, the logistic costs take up a large portion of the mutual costs of the suppliers. A mutual goal of logistic partners should therefore be to decrease logistic costs by increasing synchronic manufacturing and avoiding multiple storage sites. It must be decided where storage should be concentrated and whether storage capacities could be reduced or less used.

The cooperative partners can agree to have the entire optimization of the logistic system between supplier and manufacturer in a mutual project group. For this, a project mediator can be used whose goal is to decrease the system costs. Master plans that usually present project routines as an input-output model of defined variables are not used in the mediation of project groups that extend beyond individual companies. The momentum that usually sets in during project routines can be actively supported according to a *planned evolution* and catalyzed with supporting measures. For the planning and introduction of an intelligent integral logistics concept, a project group is first put together from the representatives of cooperative partners. The strategy is to mediate the project group with the help of an ideal typical project routine plan to serve as a guideline. The plan is detailed in Figure 4.2.

In project groups, the common goals extending beyond individual companies must first be defined. Following this, hard and soft restrictions are discussed and analyzed. Depending on the partners' preferences, the restrictions are placed in preferential order. In order to judge the future logistics chain, case scenarios are finally designed. To achieve a better transparency for the later cost assignment, all company-specific restrictions (e.g., storage facilities in an

FIGURE 4.2. Project Routine Plan

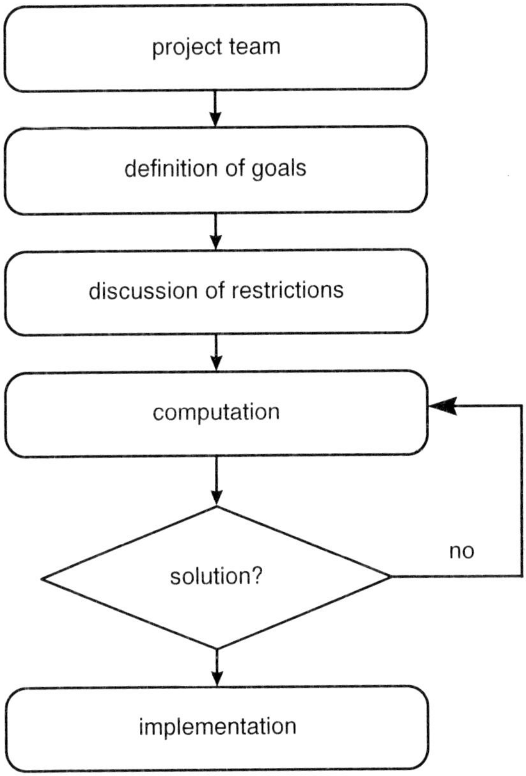

unfavorable location, interdependency with other customers of the supplier, demands of the workers, council members, etc.) are neglected in the first analytical scenario. An optimum solution is sought with the help of a formal planning instrument. Then every restriction is discussed in the previously determined order, to decide whether it is absolutely necessary. If one partner insists on a consideration, a new scenario is defined, and following this, an optimum solution is sought. The resulting cost difference is picked up by the insisting party. The new scenario is then further examined. This process is reiterated until all restrictions have been discussed. The temporary solution is discussed. If the discussion finds that the tentative solution could get the approval of both parties, it is included in the group of solutions with a potential for consensus.

Since interdependencies exist between the restrictions, the order in which the restrictions are discussed influences the cost assignment. Hence a consensus must be found not only for the order, but also with interdependent restrictions, for the cost assignment. Due to the clear decisional interdependence and the sensitivity to the sequence, the process is reiterated in different orders. The solutions with the best consensus potentials are collected. These make up the basis for further negotiations. Both parties propose an offer to split the costs for each of the solutions. In final discussions a solution is chosen and a division of cost takes place.

The process does not necessarily and absolutely lead to a solution, since the agreement of both parties is always required. It guarantees however, that a good information exchange between the partners occurs by discussing a multitude of scenarios, and thus makes the partners aware of the hard and soft restrictions. A solution reached in this manner makes it possible for both parties to realize cost decreases and to successfully implement the logistics concept.

Case Example: Mitsubishi Motors

In many industries, vertical integration is giving way to virtual integration. Toyota's decision to release Nippondenso from its production network is part of the Japanese auto industry's shift toward "modular production," where prefabricated chunks with scores of parts are supplied by outsiders and bolted together at the last minute.

Within the Mitsubishi-*keiretsu*, the automobile industry is represented by Mitsubishi Motors. Mitsubishi Motors can be grouped together with Honda and Mazda in the group of the medium-large automobile manufacturers behind the large manufacturers, Toyota and Nissan. Similar to the practice of other manufacturers, the suppliers are bound into a vertical production and delivery structure. Delivery structures are mostly characterized by exclusiveness, whereby the classic delivery structures have made room for more flexibly held and loosely connected distribution structures. The transformation of vertical production *keiretsu* into permeable networks made Mitsubishi Motors carry out uniformly the logistical sequences in the future, with the participation of all partners and mutual analysis of the necessary system costs.

Some of Mitsubishi Motors' suppliers make modules assembled at Mitsubishi Motors' plants. Some experts such as Banerji and Sambharya (1996), and Kim, Nishiguchi, and Lynn (1997) believe Japanese manufacturers will eventually sell off their engine and auto assembly plants. As virtual integration evolves, futurists such as Naisbitt (1994) envision a time when product developers, manufacturers, and distributors will be so tightly linked through data networks that inventory will all but disappear. Companies will make goods based on the daily needs of retailers. Even automobiles will be assembled to a customer's specifications within days, just as Toshiba and NEC do now with computers. A sunset industry no longer, manufacturing will help drive innovation.

One of the suppliers of Mitsubishi Motors produces electronic components for the company and also for two other Japanese manufacturers. It has a main plant and two smaller production sites that specifically manufacture small- and medium-size quantities for the newly added automobile manufacturers. The main site is in immediate proximity to Mitsubishi Motors, which used to have a gross income share of 70 percent of the total volume of the main site. The ordered components used to be products that were manufactured in large quantities. The flow of material runs from the supplier to Mitsubishi Motors, while the information flow runs from Mitsubishi Motors to the supplier.

Mitsubishi Motors used three sites, which were supplied with parts by the supplier. The main manufacturing site had a storage facility on the property close to the production site and a geographically close temporary storage facility with a hauling contractor. The production storage site was used for accounting purposes exclusively serviced through the hauling storage. The two other sites each had smaller storage areas closer to the manufacturing sites, which were serviced directly by the smaller sites of the supplier as well as by the hauling storage.

Mitsubishi Motors and the supplying companies have agreed to stop the obvious multiple storaging and to utilize the saved costs. Mitsubishi Motors aimed to decrease the storage to a necessary limit, so that the delivery terms and deadlines could be kept. Furthermore the storage facilities close to the manufacturer were to be enlarged so that the storage facility with the hauling contractor could be abandoned and the storage facility with the supplier could be given up. In connection with these changes, the storage facility close to the manufacturing site was to be maintained by the supplier and the main storage facility was to be built specifically by the supplier.

The supplier, on the other hand, wanted to continue to use its main storage site, since this already had a good infrastructure and the fixed costs needed to be maintained anyway, even if it was abandoned. Furthermore, the supplier did not want to maintain a storage site close to the manufacturer, since this could prove to be inflexible in regard to other customers. The described ideas of the logistic partners were obviously conflicting with each other. The mutual goal of lowering costs still remained. Mitsubishi Motors, after extensive discussions, could then be convinced that prescribed solutions that left no decreasable fixed costs for the supplier could not be a good solution for either company. The companies agreed to tackle integral optimization of the logistic system in a mutual project group, shown in Figure 4.3.

Through the various iterations during the mediated course of the project, the ideal goals of the logistic partners were brought closer together. After intensive discussions of the hard and soft restrictions it became clear that the solution favored by Mitsubishi Motors would lead to fixed costs that could not be diminished, and thus to extra costs. In sum, only a minimal cost reduction could have therefore been achieved. During the course of the discussion the interests

FIGURE 4.3. Optimized Logistics Concept

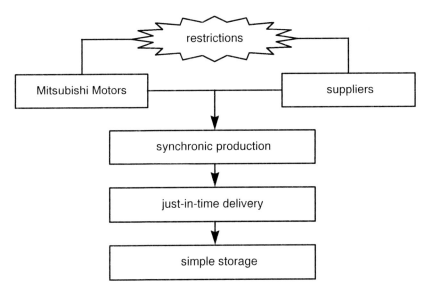

of the supplier were put forward. However, the solution favored by the supplier also led to no improvement of the status quo. By assigning costs according to restriction demands of the partners, the supplier was able to realize the less than optimal result of its preferred solution.

During the course of the discussion, Mitsubishi Motors refrained from its demand to erect the previously seen as necessary storage facilities exclusively on their property. The supplier's previous investment in its main storage site was too high to consider discontinuation of use as a conceivable concept. Due to the close proximity of both main sites, the main storage facility of the supplier could carry out the desired commissioner's function of the supply parts, so that they could do without the new main storage facility that was to be built. The responsibility to keep deadlines was taken on by the supplier in the main storage site. From the optimized logistics concept, substantial savings of relevant costs along the entire logistics chain were estimated by the partners. A fair sharing of costs was discussed and decided on for the project management to correspond to the savings and the logistics chain.

The procedure of an integral optimization of the logistics chain gave substantial cost and competition advantages at Mitsubishi Motors and with the supplier, since the companies were attuned to each other in a close partnership and their knowledge through logistical courses between the companies was exclusive. Aside from the physical flow of material, the interaction also had a substantial influence on the flow of information. The partners had to adapt their manufacturing procedures to the changed flow of materials. The supplier company used the change to introduce a new software system. According to the supplier's estimate, the initial investment for the purchase and the training will have paid for itself after half a year, since the flow of information is now much more effective and quicker, and leads to a shorter cycle time.

TECHNOLOGY COOPERATION

The multilayered formations of strategic networks in Japan contributed greatly to the technological advances in the 1980s and 1990s, which were especially evident in the development in the area of microelectronics. In hindsight this development, according to Miyashita and Russel (1994), can be linked particularly to R&D expenditures within the network association of Japanese companies from various market industries. The developmental efforts of many companies had to be coordinated, for which the association structure of the *keiretsu* seemed especially suitable and these, as Nakatani (1990) is convinced, have greater synergies in comparison to R&D services within a classical conglomerate structure. Zeleny, Cornet, and Stoner (1990) also aim in the same direction with their concept of a systemic netting: high-tech industries that want to be able to match the demands of microelectronics must undergo a systems linking with other market areas in addition to having substantial financial means at their disposal. The developments in the area of microelectronics have led to a strong push in technology that strengthened the trend for rationalization through the division of work to the technological integration. Thus one can observe that telecommunication, computer technology, and manufacturing techniques have grown together. This development is seen as integration technology in systems technology. Competition between single industrial branches becomes transparent and begins to overlap. Companies can no longer occupy the border area of their own competencies and thus try to achieve the necessary expertise through cooperative agreements (DeBresson and Amesse, 1991; Baker, 1992). This process differs from the classic form of diversification in which technology fields are linked, often without a content connection.

With rising costs, a shift occurs from variable to fixed costs (Anderson, Hakansson, and Johanson, 1994). In the development of storage chips, huge investment efforts become necessary that often cannot be borne by a single company. The coverage of fixed costs to receive returns on investments forces companies to take on global strategies, such as the formation of technology cooperatives with competitors. Thus the paradox develops that competitors mutually develop products since they are no longer able to do so by themselves.

The time factor accelerates the process of the technological systems integration and the rising volume of investments. Thus time becomes a new dimension of competition (Drucker, 1993). The quick technological advance and shortened product life cycles force companies to react more quickly to developments that they themselves have brought about. The time spiral leads to a strengthening of the above-described processes and leads to an increase of companies in strategic networks.

System integration, increasing investment amounts, and the time factor make cooperation in the form of technology alliances more sensible. Technology alliances are cooperatives that bring technology resources of the cooperating companies together. These are either created through contracted arrangements, through the exchange of research results, or through the concrete establishment of mutual research and development labs. Production and marketing of the mutually developed products are usually done by the participating companies themselves. The strategic goal of technology cooperatives is to share the costs and risks of product development (Laage-Hellman, 1997). By sharing costs and risks, a possible wrong outcome can be mutually carried by all participating companies. The individual risk for a company can thus be decreased.

Economic transactions through the market do not require companies to split resources. All other activities in which technology generation is most important can be seen as the beginning of a technology cooperative. For example, limited resource sharing can encompass licensing, cross-licensing, research of orders, etc. Characterizing resources changes substantially if capital participation enters the game. The financial exchange of shares between the partners leads to the rethinking of the basic rules of the cooperative and to giving shares only to a few selected partners.

Shortage of Resources

Due to Japan's late economic development at the beginning of the Meiji period, companies had to build up an industrial structure comparable to Western industrial countries with a relatively limited amount of resources. With the first economic developmental push at the end of the nineteenth century, Japanese companies signed cooperative agreements with companies of different manufacturing levels. Consequently, the historical processes led to Japanese companies concentrating on their specific abilities. Simultaneously, functional interorganizational cooperatives had to be established for obtaining resources and supplier parts, for distribution, and, increasingly, for product development. This was necessary for long-term survival in light of the chronic limitations of resources.

Even after the companies' structures had stabilized in the postwar years, Japanese companies still remained relatively smaller than their Western equivalents. This was due to the companies' internal resources being limited and the companies being dependent on foreign production techniques. Because of this, a backward integration was out of the question and ideas for progress failed due to the already established inner Japanese distribution net from the early days of industrialization.

The limited resources of Japanese companies can be held responsible for the development of a network of both cooperating and competing companies (Fruin, 1992). Gaps in technology must be closed due to limited resources. In doing so, the participating partners specialize in a certain job field and area of expertise. They usually invest large amounts into the business relationships, because a large part of the investment is specific to a project or cooperative.

This means it can rarely be used in any other way. As soon as one of the partners leaves the agreement, the investments of the other companies can become irrelevant (Santos Antonio, 1999). The partners in technology cooperatives are dependent on one another, since they each are in charge of critical resources.

The idea of limited disposal of critical resources was first formulated by Penrose (1959), who viewed companies as organizations for the accumulation of human and material resources. This assumption was further developed in the so-called resource dependency approach (Pfeffer and Salancik, 1978). The basic assumption is that organizations are exposed to limited resources. They can purchase these resources from other organizations. In order to gain control over resources, two basic strategies can be used. First, companies can absorb all endangering sources through acquisition. If a company lacks technologies that are important for its survival, and has only limited time to develop these technologies within the organization, the company, if it has sufficient financial resources, can acquire the one that has the technology available. Second, companies can try to decrease uncertainties through cooperation strategies. Pfeffer and Salancik recommend the cooperation strategy, if the cooperating companies have a clear mutual interest.

The resource dependency approach is less about material resources such as assets, buildings, production machines, raw materials, etc., which are generally accessible and available. In a strategic perspective, the focus is on distinctive or critical resources such as skills, necessary expertise, reputation for customer loyalty, and company-specific assets such as patents, licenses, concessions, trademarks, and copyrights (Peteraf, 1993). Companies have a competitive advantage only by "being different" (Grant, 1991; Mahoney and Pandian, 1992).

By integrating into a strategic network, companies catapult themselves from a position of limited resources into a structure with potential resources. With the entrance into a network, a relative surplus of resources is manifested that can provoke inefficiency, but, if used wisely, can also help secure company goals. If viewed separately, Japanese companies suffer from a chronic limitation of resources. The integration into strategic networks, however, provides abundant critical resources.

Limitations in resources can be overcome by bringing together the resources of two or more companies. According to the degree of mutual commitment and implicit dependency, three types of resource linking can be distinguished: technical meetings, rotation of R&D personnel, and pooling of R&D labs (see Figure 4.4).

Technical meetings are necessary for the formation of resource linking, which leaves the autonomy of the companies mostly intact. Researchers of all cooperating companies meet periodically to exchange R&D results. Depending on the trust and intensity of the interaction, companies can direct and influence the flow of information. In the next step, companies can begin to exchange R&D personnel. In mutual, time-limited development projects, researchers come together and are, for a period of time, assigned to the cooperative partners. The most involved form of technological cooperation is the pooling of R&D labs in the form of R&D consortia, joint venture, etc. All three types of R&D cooperation between companies are structures to link critical resources to cooperative partners. With this, the central leading task is to recognize the potential of resource linking within the strategic network early on, to combine them and take care of them (Van de Ven, Walker, and Liston, 1979). The model idea of resource shortage and resource combination forms the basis for a system of methodical concepts of systemic technology management.

Systemic Technology Management

The word technology is often used in current economic discussions, but is also used with different meanings. The broadest, mutual base can be interpreted as user knowledge or as skill. In its original sense, the word stems from the Greek art of industrial

FIGURE 4.4. Linking of Resources

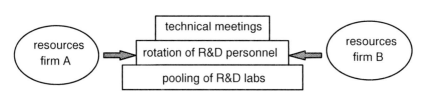

manufacturing of objects. Today the term technology is normally used in the sense of knowledge about technological innovations, to the extent that this knowledge is used for solving practical problems, such as the development of products and processes (Dosi, 1988; Hagedoorn and Schakenraad, 1994). If technology is utilized science, then not only can the sciences make up the basis for technological disciplines, e.g., physics for the sciences and biology for medicine, but also the social sciences (Popper, 1963). Technology in its broadest interpretation therefore also encompasses Popper's definition of technology.

The characteristics of a company integrated into a network association can be seen in the change from a conventional, more operative innovation management to a strategically stronger and systems-oriented technology management. Technology management goes beyond innovation management as it does not just deal with technological innovation, but also with directing developments, keeping and using technology competencies over the life span of technologies. It deals with the new as well as already existing technologies. The change from innovation management to technology management is shown in Figure 4.5.

FIGURE 4.5. From Innovation Management to Technology Management

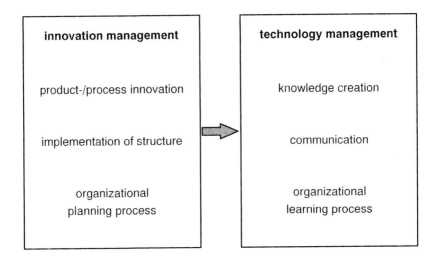

The goal of conventional innovation management is to bring out concrete, mostly incremental product and process innovations (Hippel, 1988). The employees of a business unit are working on the development of new products and achievements, whereby their tasks are ideally implemented in a specific organizational structure. The responsibility for innovation processes lies less with corporate management and more in the technical functional areas. The companies concentrate on innovations within the organizational boundaries and protect themselves from competitors. Innovation management means, first and foremost, planning of technological output. It uses methods such as portfolio analysis and budgeting. A relatively rigid order of logically aligned developmental steps is supposed to suggest the relevance of good planning.

Because of inherent formal structures, conventional innovation management is more of a hindrance than a help for the layout of innovative processes in turbulent economic times (Drucker, 1980, 1993; Senge, 1993). According to their nature, innovations are the result of a creative search for a competitive differentiation and thus not plannable in detail. Rather, they can be guided along the principles of a planned evolution in the tension field between stability and flexibility. Dosi (1988) believes that innovations result from technological paradigms and run continuously as technological trajectories in specific context-dependent lanes, because they primarily result from cumulative, gradual learning processes. In building technological paradigms, influences such as the needs of customers, competition, and integrated cooperative partners in a strategic network play an essential role next to new scientific knowledge.

Systemic technology management encompasses the entire decisional process, which is focused on the development and the use of knowledge for new products and processes and therefore does not allow itself to be reduced to traditional use of innovations. Systemic technology management initiates the permanent generation and use of knowledge through organizational learning in a permeable organization system. Such organizations seek cooperatives between companies with suppliers, customers, and competitors, in order to derive new technologies. Cooperatives are being used to integrate the knowledge of other companies into their own knowledge base. Systemic technology management thus does not make planning models available, but sees the building of new products and businesses as a multidimensional learning and innovation process. The idea is thus especially pragmatic and yet still available for change. It is based on the worry for the availability of knowledge and leads to a constant, active readiness to change organizations.

A systemic technology management focuses on the three fields of knowledge: innovations, competencies, and culture. The final measurable output—innovations—is only the tip of the iceberg within a linked learning process. Vertical learning processes are connected with horizontal learning processes and thus have an ability to connect to the knowledge resources that are hidden in the strategic network. Successful technology management demands a corporate culture that rewards creativity and innovations. Companies that are technology leaders in their markets obviously have enormous excitement for technology that is not just limited to the closer R&D area, but rather applies across all functions. Beyond the functional areas, competencies from which innovations can be derived must be built.

The availability of a clear strategy concept, from which the role of technology management emerges, is certainly a key factor in the generation of knowledge. For this, visions as directional pointers of strategic intentions and efforts play an important role, especially if the evolution of technological trajectories and the development of resulting business potentials is not yet visible (Mattsson, 1987; Alevsson and Berg, 1992; Czarniawska-Joerges, 1992; Powell, Koput, and Smith-Doerr, 1996). Visions can function as goals and can at the same time be catalysts for the unfolding of goal-oriented tasks.

Case Example: Fujitsu

Successful technology leaders such as Fujitsu, Sony, and Canon cultivate and improve their technology competency and see it as the basis for a continuous flow of innovations. In comparison to their less successful competitors, they market two to three times as many new products, use two to three times as many technologies, are more than twice as fast in the introduction of a new product, and compete in twice as many product and regional markets (Neves, Summe, and Utal, 1990). Fujitsu can be used as an example of effective technology management. Like other companies of the electronics and telecommunications industries in the early 1990s, Fujitsu was faced with the problem of stagnant world markets in the conventional businesses, while large initial investments were necessary to enter the highly promising new markets that developed from the merging of the electronics and telecommunications industries.

New business openings required a systematic search process that began with the analysis of existing business potential. On the basis of kept competencies, possible areas of growth and future development were analyzed. The selection of promising success fields that were searched on the criteria of market attractiveness and competitive strength built the foundation for a derivative of market strategies and the realization of multiple transactions. Fujitsu was pursuing the goal of combining technological knowledge of the electronics and telecommunications industries and deriving new products from these (Teramoto et al., 1994). The organizational integration of new business units was accomplished in R&D labs that were supported jointly due to resource sharing.

Since the early 1990s, Fujitsu has entered several cooperative agreements with companies such as Advanced Micro Devices (AMD), Siemens, Sun Microsystems, Olicom, Bay Networks, etc., which all lie in the spectrum between the electronics and telecommunications industries. Fujitsu operated very successfully within this cooperative network (Celeste, 1996) and was able to receive significant new innovations with the corresponding competencies. The question is why the technology management practiced by Fujitsu led to relatively successful results. The cooperative strategy behind Fujitsu is shown in Figure 4.6.

Fujitsu follows a cooperative strategy that is made for the entire company. Two problems need to be solved: one is in which production field the company should be active and the second, how the headquarters can lead the entire business areas. Such an orientation characterizes Fujitsu as an organization that represents more than just the sum of single business areas. Potential cooperative partners are selected based on their usefulness in certain business areas and for the entire company. A cooperative partner does not always bring a directly measurable benefit to a certain business area, but rather for the company as a whole. The headquarters, with its connected

FIGURE 4.6. Network Planning

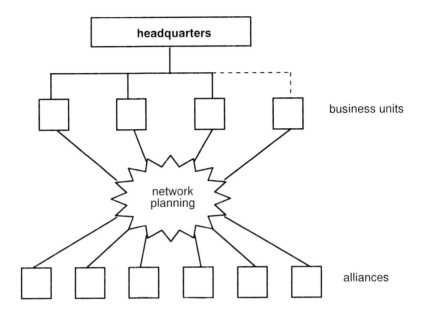

departments and the concerned business department, usually bring the cooperation agreements together.

Network planning is the term used by Fujitsu to describe the process in which the business units and the headquarters vote about cooperative goals. It is clear that the output of an alliance cannot be specifically planned but rather is influenced by cooperative partners and the market. Nonetheless, Fujitsu sets a goal for every cooperative agreement that is supposed to set a benchmark for the possible cooperative success in a best-case scenario. During the course of the cooperative a mediation occurs between the goal and the opportunities that arise from the learning processes. Network planning often can be followed by several R&D alliances that are contracted with one cooperative partner. The cooperative partner is thus linked to several business areas.

Porter (1987) calls the organizational strategy behind the idea of network planning *corporate strategy.* In contrast, a *business unit strategy* tries to achieve competitive advantages in every business area in which a company is active. Teramoto et al. (1994) have realized that Fujitsu's cooperative strategy is closely linked to the organizational strategy of the company. Business areas and departments are not separated to the extent that they are in Western companies. The responsibilities are loosely defined and the boundaries between the organizational units are fluid. For certain tasks, project teams are created in which employees of different departments come together. The teams work on projects that entail the planning, development, production, and extend to the marketing of the products, thus guaranteeing optimum teamwork and a steady exchange of information between the employees of the different organizational units. The project teams sometimes only exist a short time. After fulfilling a certain goal, the teams are dissolved again.

Fujitsu's loose order of organizational units is reminiscent of Weick's *loosely coupled systems* (Weick, 1976; Orton and Weick, 1990). Loosely coupled systems are systems that are not subdivided according to hierarchy and whose subdivisions interact and communicate with one another, while retaining their independence and identity. Weick claims that his idea is not just an organizational concept for the management of companies. Loosely coupled systems are more like structures to solve problems in complex systems in general. In this sense Fujitsu is a loosely coupled system and acts as such. The organizational units of the company dissolve from time to time and recombine into new units and teams. They often maintain their identity and return to their original form. Interactions between the departments lead to temporarily existing organizational units or even to new departments.

Fujitsu's business unit for work stations originally stemmed from a project team that was integrated into a cooperative with the American company Sun Microsystems. The project team turned out to be so successful that it could be transferred into a new business area. With the assembling of project teams, Fujitsu follows the goal of entering product areas with high growth potential. The structure of a loosely coupled system serves Fujitsu as the basis of a differentiated cooperative strategy with increased knowledge, within the setting of a systemic technology management.

GLOBALIZATION COOPERATION

The basic conditions of economic life have fundamentally changed since the beginning of the 1990s. Geographical economic areas as company's fields of action have continuously increased with the elimination of customs barriers and with increasing purchasing power of the customers. World brands achieve more importance, so that supranational consumer groups develop with very similar consumer behavior. In a time of increased international competition for cost and innovation, one must rethink the regional distribution of the value chain and consider changed competencies and limited activities. Companies try to achieve globalization in almost all capacities. Globalization is almost synonymous for shifting the entire value chain beyond the former home markets.

Japan is no longer an inexpensive manufacturing site; it is among the most expensive manufacturing sites in the world. The high production costs in the country, the increasing political trade difficulties as well as the massively increasing currency (*endaka*) since the early 1990s, have led to the construction of production sites outside Japan. Until recently, the Asian neighboring countries were merely a cheap reservoir of labor for Japanese transplants. Now increasingly the entire value chain is being brought there, as well as to Europe and North America. This hollowing-out phenomenon means that Japanese companies must globalize in order to forgo the cost trap of production in their home country (Noguchi, 1993; Itami, 1994; Tselichtchev, 1999). Japan is no special case, but is in tune with all Western industrial nations that are falling into the globalization trap. Business opportunities are increasingly vanishing for companies that do not undergo globalization efforts. Only globalized companies that have the necessary financial resources to build manufacturing sites in other countries have a chance for survival in a deregulated global economic order (Thurow, 1996). Today Japan's economy is endangered primarily by Southeast Asian companies whose home market once served as the first globalization step for many Japanese companies. Taiwanese, Thai, Malaysian, and Korean companies have learned from their former teachers and are now relentlessly pushing into the markets that Japanese companies have been able to conquer and defend since the late 1970s.

Globalization does not just occur to reduce costs and to balance the exchange rates. Only through a broad scattering of company activities can they maintain their ability to compete in the long run on a worldwide scale. It is not just about the building of a manufacturing plant in a foreign country. That can merely be the first step. The goal of globalization is the internationalization of all corporate functions (Barlett and Ghoshal, 1987). Local development teams with their specific technological competencies can be linked and synergistically bound worldwide. If changing tendencies in the need structures can be recognized and used due to the presence in that country, then the matching products can be placed onto that market very quickly. Thus, globalization is about activating knowledge potentials spread around the globe and to make them accessible for the company. To be directly in a country means to be able to use local resources and have a direct entrance to that market.

In the meantime, Japanese companies are orientating themselves more and more often on the international market as a production site and are intensifying the focus to internationalize locally available resources. The globalization of Japanese companies leaves open the question about efficiency of network cooperatives. The ethnic and cultural homogeneity, as found in the combining of mutual resources in domestic networks could turn out to be a boomerang on the ethnically and culturally diverse world economy, despite the help of an open flow of information between the member companies and the support of the trading houses and banks. Can Japanese companies stand up to this diversity?

Japanese scientists as well as businessmen have been pondering this question for a long time: Can the Japanese way of interfirm cooperation simply be transferred into a foreign country? (See, for example, Yoshihara, 1989; Ferguson, 1990; Park, Gunther, and Osten, 1992; Beck and Hansen, 1993; Serapio, 1995; Abo, 1995.) Indeed, management strategies abroad are as much like the idol of the Japanese home country as one egg is to another. In this context Lasserre and Schütte (1995) also refer to this as a "mini-Japan." Other authors compare the transfer of Japanese network structures to a colonization of the host country (Jackson, 1993; Yoshino and Rangan, 1995). Chikudate (1995) criticizes the immobility and inflexibility of Japanese companies in foreign countries: traditional patterns of behavior are simply instilled in the foreign business environment without critically respecting its latent differences. Scher (1997), on the other hand, believes that the island mentality, which was still part of Japanese companies long after the economic miracle of the postwar years, was successfully unlearned and transformed into an extremely open business strategy, oriented toward the worldwide mobilization of knowledge resources. Nonaka (1990) and Dirks (1994, 1995) see the globalization of Japanese companies as a self-renewing process: Japanese companies can learn new behavioral forms during the building up of production sites, research institutions, and cooperative agreements. Japanese firms may evolve as a new type of multicultural organization in the near future. An evaluation of Japanese globalization efforts can therefore be quite controversial. The globalization of Japanese companies seems to be closely linked with the legacy of network cooperation.

Companies in Global Competition

The increasing globalization of the economy undermines one of the fundamental posts of the nation-state, the national market. The nation-state as the most important strategic economic area is being replaced by the emerging global area of competing and cooperating firms. However, that does not mean that the power of the nation-state is becoming obsolete, nor that nation-states in their economic spheres are being replaced by transnational companies. The national prosperity is less and less dependent on the success of the companies at home, e.g., on their technologies, their assets, or their labor force. However, companies are becoming more and more important as part of a global network which reacts to strategic interests that are not directly linked to those of the nation-state. Naisbitt (1994) even holds that traditional cultural and ethnic differences will re-emerge as a force that will weaken existing nation-states. The existing political leadership will be found inadequate for the new economic age. Prosperity is, on the contrary, more dependent on technologies that were developed and produced in other parts of the world, on assets that can be used on the global market, and increasingly on qualified labor whose education has taken place in other countries.

Against the background of the failure of nation-state politics for the development of national economies, the question arises as to how national economic development should be organized and how the necessary capacities and abilities should be released. Successful national economic development and the creation of new work are increasingly based on the differences and independence of single companies while at the same time cooperating for mutual use in a given geographical area. In this takeover process of previous state functions, for example, through global strategic networks, capacities and abilities are unfolded that are important for a self-organized and long-term directed economic development.

Globalization and the contrasting concept—localization—probably belong on the list of the most catchy and omnipresent buzzwords of the present economic debate. Globalization describes the necessity to become active on the world market to secure further company growth and the international ability for competition (Henzler and Rall, 1986; Barlett and Ghoshal, 1987; Gupta and Govindarajan, 1991; Thurow, 1996). Companies, as part of a progressive defense, have to open up future areas of growth in global competition. At the same time they have to take up impulses from these growth areas and work them through.

Localization, on the other hand, indicates a recollection of the local home market that in the past used to be responsible for generating competencies and manufacturing products. It is true that territory as a defining concept will become increasingly meaningless. The process of globalization, as Naisbitt (1994) argues, will not necessarily be smooth. In the age of globalization, the value chain activities on the home market are questioned sooner or later, since a shifting of partial activities into the foreign country from a cost and market point of view makes sense. From this, an increase in unemployment in the home country results, since certain activities of the value chain disappear with no substitute. The traditional instruments of economic navigation can no longer work with increasing globalization, since ways for a new global navigation are only partially discussed and still seem to be far from being implemented in the form of "world contracts." Single economies thus increasingly close themselves off from the world market and stand, fired up by protagonists of a national economy that call upon the limits of competition and curse the negative signs of globalization against any globalization wishes of their home companies (Group of Lisbon 1995, Krugman 1995). The opposition toward the dictatorship of worldwide markets has grown louder and the volume will continue to rise.

At first glance, the catchwords of globalization and localization seem to stand for opposite directions. Globalization works with centrifugal force, localization with centripetal force. Globalization is generally associated with open borders, an open mind and—in an economic context—with open markets. Localization, on the other hand, is associated with local patriotism, nostalgia, and protectionism. Kidd (1994) shows in his study of Japanese production sites in England that only a few large companies practice globalization and localization in the extreme. A successful globalization also requires tough roots in a home market, from which global advances can occur. Turned around, globalization can always be a prerequisite for localization. Only a strong global presence can bring out the roots of a company in its specific geographic-cultural environment. Globalization works through localization. Nonaka (1990) and Müller (1997) have similar opinions that the assimilation of multicultural aspects of global competition and embedding the global into the local play a central role in generating competitive advantage.

Kanter (1995) holds that sweeping changes in the competitive landscape, including the presence of foreign competitors in domestic markets, are driving businesses to rethink their strategies and structures to reach beyond traditional boundaries. Increasing numbers of small and midsize companies are joining corporate giants in striving to exploit international growth markets or in trying to become world class even if only to retain local customers.

In this sense the mutual reference of globalization and localization is an oxymoron. The opposite poles of globalization and localization can be reconciled through a dialectic alignment: companies have foremost a local geographical background and have been formed by many cultural influences. Globalization and localization are weighed against each other and synthesized. Figure 4.7 shows companies in the potential triangle of global developmental possibilities, which are to be brought in accordance with a specific sociocultural background.

FIGURE 4.7. Globalization in the Context of Organizational Learning

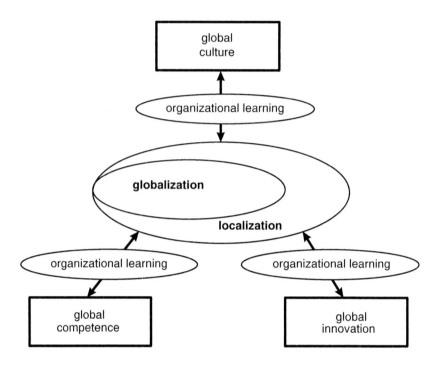

Globalization always occurs from the tradition of past corporate evolution and is thus tightly bound to the localization of the company on a home market and its specific culture. The synthetic connection between globalization and localization is reflected in the three levels of knowledge: culture, competence, and innovation. Knowledge is global insofar as it is available in all major areas of the strategic network of a company (Nonaka and Takeuchi, 1995; Fedor and Werther, 1995). In this sense, culture as one of the three levels of knowledge is just as much a continuous production as a continuously changing product. This unconsciously also suggests that individual cultural identity can be kept during the adaptation process to other cultures, because whoever gets involved in a foreign culture will possibly also be seen as a "foreigner" in comparison to his or her own previous culture. It is not surprising that Sony, for example, is considered more "American" than a traditional Japanese firm. This cultural typology, as Chikudate (1996) points out, is due to early globalization of the company in North America.

Global competencies are just as much part of the repertoire of successful companies as global innovations. The ability to establish competencies around the globe and to extract innovations from these is a challenge of the first order. It is important that the globally accumulative knowledge potentials can be balanced against existing competencies and innovations with the help of vertical and horizontal learning. In contrast to the accumulation of knowledge on the home market, this balancing, which can be also termed "socialization," plays a far more important role (Kanter, 1995). Such a boundary that spans socialization is time consuming and costly, but indispensable for further globalization.

International Alliances

The character of international alliances has fundamentally changed. In the past, international alliances were primarily formed in order to forgo legal restrictions on a certain geographical market. In this fashion, countries that established protective industrial politics allow only restricted direct investments and suggest joint ventures between foreign investors and local firms as investment alternatives. In place of such joint ventures whose goal is to enter the local market, today alliances are more often entered by equal companies that are possibly both active in related fields (Yip, 1992). Companies that form alliances across borders due to their globalization strategies do not limit their cooperative by catering to a single market, but strive for global cooperation.

Globalization today is a trunk, or partial, globalization. *Triadization* is thus a more fitting description of the current situation. Triadization means that the technological, economic, and social cultural integration processes between the three most developed regions of the world—Japan, Western Europe, and North America—are more permeable, more intensive and more significant than the integration between these three regions and the less-developed countries, or among the disadvantaged countries themselves (Ohmae, 1985; Davidow and Malone, 1992). The so-called triad of Japan, Western Europe, and North America forms a single consumer market. Lifestyle and consumers' demands are becoming more similar. Companies are increasingly coordinating their activities on the triad markets in order to reach consumers worldwide and to maintain their competitive ability. According to Ohmae (1989), strategic networks are a suitable medium to serve the triad completely. Geographically remote areas are especially suitable for the formation of strategic networks. Of all network cooperatives worldwide, over 90 percent are contracted from Japan, Western Europe, and North America (Roche, 1996). In Figure 4.8, company networks are depicted in triadization form.

A radically new competitive strategy forces the companies to introduce their products on all important markets simultaneously. Ohmae illustrates this by using the example of market introduction of the video recorder in the second half of the 1970s (Ohmae, 1985; Kotter, 1997). Sony, Matsushita, and Philips brought video recorders onto the market at about the same time. Sony brought out the Betamax, Matsushita the VHS, and Philips the video recorder 2000. The three appliances had different standards. The consumer could only play tapes made for that certain appliance. A self-inducing spiral effect thus began. The more appliances that were sold, the

FIGURE 4.8. Networking As Triadization

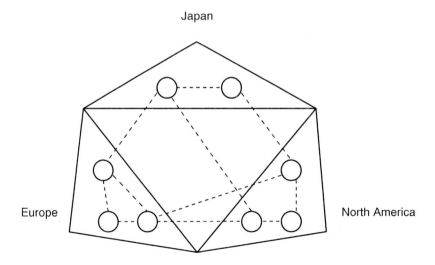

more cassette tapes were manufactured for them, and the more appliances were thus again sold. The competition became a fierce fight for the standard.

From the beginning, Matsushita and Sony went beyond their Japanese home market into the American and European market. Matsushita conquered a 15 percent market share in the United States with the help of its own distribution organization, and another 45 percent with the help of OEM distributions to various American manufacturers and distribution partners. A similar picture developed for Matsushita in Europe. Sony used the same strategy of sales via subsidiaries and via strategic networks, but was far behind Matsushita in terms of market shares. Philips limited itself to the European home market. This quickly led to the video recorder 2000 vanishing from the market. The dispute was reduced to a dual fight between Matsushita and Sony, that Matsushita finally decided for itself—thanks to the speed with which Matsushita simultaneously conquered all three markets of the triad.

This example shows how companies today are confronted with changed competitive situations. In the past, a company introduced a new product stepwise onto one market after another. It first opened up the home market, from there it went to the markets of other industrialized nations, and finally entered the third world markets. In modern high technology markets, however, no time remains for such a "cascade strategy." Here, the company wins that can market the new product immediately and simultaneously over the entire triad. The company that remains limited to its home market eventually even loses that market to its global competitors (Kanter, 1995). Unlike the past, a company can no longer stay successful on a national level if it is not globally successful as well (Davidow and Malone, 1992). The national market disintegrates into a world market. Globalization becomes a condition of survival.

Globally acting companies form global network alliances with partners from the triad. The partners mutually market their products on the corresponding home markets. Every partner completes its line of products and at the same time better utilizes its own distribution apparatus. The partners exchange complementary technologies and perform R&D together. They establish joint companies on their home markets and in third world countries. In this way global network cooperatives become a central element in the competitive strategy. The ability to find partners and successfully manage a strategic network becomes one of the most important skills of a company.

Most strategic networks, not just those of the Japanese, are increasingly turning into global networks as a result of the ongoing globalization of markets, products, and labor. According to Lorange and Ross (1992), companies usually prefer international cooperatives over the founding of subsidiaries. Thus globalization is a process based on worldwide operating strategic networks, whose capital is increasingly held by a variety of shareholders in various countries, whose culture is open, and who follow global strategies. It is difficult to recognize the specific legal, economic, and technological territories of networks even if they have a sort of "home base." This is hindered by intensive interfirm connection and integration.

Case Example: Nissan

Since the devaluation of the Thai baht in 1997, the fast-growing open economies of Asia have been roiled by a series of currency, stock market, and banking crises. No country on the Pacific Rim has been spared—even Japan, whose global industrial might has been undermined by the government's reluctance to jettison its policy. And with the Asian locomotive running in reverse, all the open economies of the emerging nations—from Latin America to Eastern Europe—have been hit hard. These shocks will not end globalization but are stark evidence of its double-edged nature. As Yip notes, short of war or an epidemic of market-closing internal policies, most countries in the twenty-first century are likely to keep pursuing globalization despite the minuses (Yip, 1998). Goods, labor, and capital will crisscross the globe as never before. The benefits are just too good to pass up.

The automobile industry is a colorful example for the necessity, but also the consequence of globalization. The combination of supply and demand sides depicts a business marked by decreasing room for growth and differentiation (Eads, 1990; Yip, 1992). New suppliers—manufacturers from striving automobile nations that are pushing into new segments—have drastically increased the intensity of competition. Consequently, immense overcapacities have developed in Japan, Europe, and the United States since the early 1990s. This has resulted in shrinking loyalty to brand names in favor of increasing price awareness.

The globalization of the automobile industry is still in its early stage. In the 1980s the opening of markets for imports was still strongly influenced by each country's national regulations. Many governments searched for political answers to the danger of Japanese imports and thus regulated the import numbers for Japanese cars. The Japanese auto industry is especially dependent on the world market in their exports. On the basis of this fact alone, Japanese trade politics can easily be understood. Japan defends a liberal world trade order, but wants to avoid a dramatic increase of imports to Japan.

The opinions on the globalization of the Japanese automobile industry are split. One side claims that with the increasing yen the Japanese companies are forced to invest outside their country to stay competitive (Cusumano and Takeishi, 1991; Shimokawa, 1994). These investments can contribute to world economic growth and thus be advantageous to the Japanese economy, especially if because of this the imports to Japan increase and the trade deficit decreases. It is not the fault of outside manufacturing, but rather the lack of demand within the country that stagnates car sales on the Japanese market. Japan also believes that a definite connection exists between increasing unemployment within Japan and the shift of manufacturing to the outside (Itami, 1994). Globalization of Japanese automobile manufacturers occurs at the cost of inland production, so that Japan's industrial base is slowly but surely being hollowed out.

Nissan, Japan's second largest automobile manufacturer, produced almost 3 million vehicles worldwide in 1997, and almost half the production occurred outside Japan. With a further increase in foreign production, the foreign share will have passed the 50 percent mark. Within Japan, drastic savings measures are being taken, which manifests in lower capital investments and decreasing employment. The closing of the plant in Zama in February 1995, the first closing of a Nissan plant ever, made headlines worldwide and is symptomatic of the change in Nissan from a national to a global firm. Despite enthusiasm for continuation of globalization efforts, the danger of an erosion of the knowledge base may exist. Entire value chains are shifted to foreign countries, especially to North America (U.S.A., Mexico), Europe (England) and Southeast Asia (Thailand, Malaysia, etc.), while also establishing R&D centers outside the country. With a history of stagnating market shares on the Japanese home market as well as the necessity of a larger presence outside Japan, Nissan decided at the beginning of the 1990s to install a project team to discuss and create a new corporate direction under the motto "global evolution," depicted in Figure 4.9.

The goal of the project was to place Nissan in the most important foreign markets in the top three of the nonlocal automobile manufacturers. Nissan formed a project team whose task was to point out the potential of the most important overseas markets and to analyze the current position of Nissan. Following the analysis, a selection of those markets was made that seemed to offer above-

FIGURE 4.9. Global Evolution

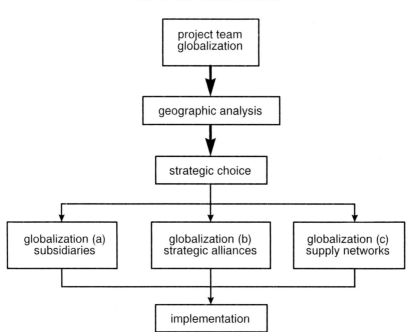

average market dynamics and realistic participation possibilities for Nissan. The selected target markets were North America, West Europe, and Southeast Asia. Not included were East Europe and Africa, while the potential of China was recognized, but currently pushed aside.

Three globalization strategies crystallized. Due to limited resources, the further establishment of subsidiaries in addition to preexisting ones in England, Spain, Mexico, and the United States was still given consideration, but globalization through strategic networks was pushed into the foreground. The option of network cooperatives as well as linking supply networks was to be pursued diligently in the future.

Nissan recognized that it had to acquire knowledge about the target markets, their cultures, and their driving habits for a thorough globalization process. It seemed obvious to staff the team with specialists who already had relevant knowledge. Particularly in the implementation phase, experienced specialists in the fields of planning, construction, production, and marketing from Europe, the United States, and Southeast Asia were invited to Japan to bring necessary experience and openness for this special task.

Today Nissan is among the Japanese automobile manufacturers that has reached the highest degree of globalization. To give an example: Nissan went into a cooperative agreement with the Korean company Samsung in 1994. The first car hit the market in 1998. This was a modified version of the Nissan Maxima. Since the Korean automobile market is still protectively closed for direct investments, the decision for a network cooperation made sense.

The case of Nissan shows that the Japanese idea of network cooperation also works outside Japan, even if some adaptations are necessary. As opposed to the network cooperation within Japan, socialization plays a much more significant role. Nissan had to reexamine innovations, competencies, and last but not least, the corporate culture and had to adapt these to the global environment. At Nissan, since the beginning phase of global evolution, the term *glocalization* is being used to describe the local component in globalization (Itami, 1991a). Glocalization does not seek to rule the local, to the contrary, it tries to point out the local as the center of global. Nissan's chairman, Kume Yukata, stated that for the sake of globalization the single Japanese automobile manufacturers as well as the suppliers within Japan should work even more closely together. Reorientation from a simultaneous assembly of equal products in the country as well as outside, in addition to building new, high quality products within Japan, requires mutual activities in regard to the rationalization of the value chain. Consequently, the link between the networks of Japanese automobile manufacturers is strengthened and not weakened, from which new competition advantages could result in the future.

The current Asian financial crisis has aggravated latent resentment against the perceived human cost of globalization, or integration into the world economy. It is a sentiment that makes International Monetary Fund-style reforms immediately suspect in the minds of many of the people they are designed to help. The crisis— in Japan as well as in other Asian countries—is breeding a form of nationalist populism that blames the region's economic plight on the "new imperialism represented by the IMF," with its message of fiscal discipline and open markets. Glocalization as an adjusted form of pure globalization seems to present an answer to the ongoing economic crisis.

Chapter 5

Entrepreneurship in the Twenty-First Century: An Outlook

During the course of discussing strategic networks, only the companies that span the network, not the individuals who make up the company, were mentioned. Indeed, it is the individuals who develop and implement network strategies (Yoshino and Rangan, 1995; Laage-Hellman, 1997). The opening of a company into a strategic network also requires the "opening" of the employees. The culturally determined frame of action is widened along a network culture, which is connected with an often painful birth of something new. The cultural exploration trip into permeable, autopoietic, and altruistic network structures that are barely navigable and are led more according to a planned evolution model requires promoters that show organizational members the advantages of a network cooperation.

Leading promoters are usually compared in the West to entrepreneurs or leaders. These are individuals that live and create a certain corporate culture in a special way. Often these promoters are identical to the founders and top managers of companies. Entrepreneurs are responsible for innovations in the economic action practice (Schumpeter, 1942). According to this view, innovation processes demand the input of economically acting individuals. They always question existing knowledge to get to untried solutions. Innovators must also possess the necessary energy to get their ideas pushed through. In this view, innovations surface during the course of a cyclic radical change of technology. Carlsson and Stankiewicz (1991) are convinced that the ideal of Schumpeter's innovative entrepreneur has influenced the corporate cultures of Western companies significantly. Entrepreneurs are

159

elevated to the status of Godlike leaders and are considered to be "heroic." Drucker (1993) demands a society of entrepreneurs in which innovations are constantly occurring.

In Japan other principles of entrepreneurship apply. The individual cannot forgo the group (Marsh and Mannari, 1986). Yasumono (1993) and Hirata and Okumura (1995) conclude that Western-style entrepreneurship is of little theoretical and empirical relevance in Japan. Charismatic entrepreneurs such as Sony's Akio Morita are more the exception than the rule, while a typical CEO in Japan is usually inconspicuous and navigates the company from the background. This is especially true in the founder of Matsushita, Konosuke Matsushita, who says that a CEO should set a moral example for his employees and should embody sincerity, modesty, and discipline (Matsushita, 1989; Kotter, 1997).

The dearth of talented entrepreneurs is a big problem is Japan. The individuals who go into venture businesses seem to be the type who can't do anything else. That is not to say that Japan lacks talent. For the most part, though, gifted engineers and executives prefer to keep their jobs at big corporations. That is because although the lifetime-employment system is starting to crumble, large companies still manage to retain their best and brightest with the lure of job security and high pay. In doing so, they discourage job mobility. Many talented engineers are trapped in large companies such as Toshiba or Fujitsu. Thus, even if they are creative or brilliant, they will not be able to realize their talents.

Japan has only produced figures of exceptional power and with revolutionary vision in times of crises. At the beginning of the Meiji period, for example, as the determinants of the social and economic order were fundamentally revised, a new caste of industrialists developed who undoubtedly helped to form the industrial revolution in Japan (Yamamura, 1971). Natural leaders are usually nowhere to be found. The Japanese prime minister, for example, has far less power than most government heads in the Western world and in most Asian countries (Reading, 1992). Also in Japanese history, important figures such as those who formed European history are scarce. This is certainly not because Japan lacks talent. Talented people are just as strongly existent as in other nations. The reason lies within the culture—individuals who elevate themselves above others are mistrusted. Bachnik (1992) sees the Japanese society as extraordinary in that it makes the full unfolding of the group possible, but only tolerates extraordinary individuals if they hide their talent in such a way as to make their accomplishments appear as accomplishments of the group. This belief helps to explain why the real power in Japan is almost always hidden in the background. Japanese society has developed an art of living together as perhaps no other nation, but in doing so the ambitions of individuals were sacrificed.

Entrepreneurs of Japanese firms usually appear without airs and graces. They understand their role more as a star among others and look for an outlet, not a confrontation. This can be seen in the fact that they make less of a distinction between their organizations than their Western equivalents, instead propagating the networking of organizations (Richter and Teramoto, 1995). In the closer circle of *keiretsu,* the presidents meet in so-called *kai,* in order to attune their company politics to one another. Also in more loosely formed cooperatives—such as the trans-*keiretsu*—a continuous exchange occurs between the members of top management. This is an indication that network cooperatives are taken seriously and are setting examples.

Teramoto, Richter, and Iwasaki (1993) notice that in network cooperatives between Japan and Western countries, the Western top management is busy mostly with legal questions about the cooperative agreement until the agreement is signed. The attitude of Japanese top management is very different. Legal and organizational questions before and at the beginning of the cooperative are trivial. Instead, it is more important to develop the cooperative in the sense of a coevolution. Japanese entrepreneurs therefore are often dismayed if they notice limited interaction with their Western counterparts after signing the contract. They take this as a lack of trust toward the joint project. The specifics of the Japanese economy can thus be seen as a constructive integration of the economic environment into the converging frame of corporate action.

FROM ENTREPRENEURSHIP TO INTERPRENEURSHIP

There are different ways to define entrepreneurship. It is important that the entrepreneur tries to give the organization some kind of structure that protects it from drifting into anarchy and chaos. Every organization must, therefore, have at least a minimal structure that defines the rules of togetherness, as most management academics will concur (e.g., Penrose, 1959; Weick, 1969; Mintzberg, 1989; Numagami, Ohta, and Nonaka, 1996; Zahra, Garvis, and George, 1999). The permanent interaction with network companies and the implicated self-dissolution of companies demands a new type of entrepreneur, one that can give the organization minimal structure without cutting into the dynamic communication processes with the organizational environment. These communication processes must be catalyzed and channeled to achieve maximum knowledge from the environment and at the same time return knowledge.

Three types of entrepreneurs can be defined that primarily fulfill the demands of organizational structure and give meaning to individual rhetoric: the classic *entrepreneur*, the *intrapreneur,* and, certainly only hypothetical, the *interpreneur.* These three concepts must be checked for usefulness in the management of strategic networks and must be evaluated regarding where to place them.

Schumpeter (1934, 1942) sketches a type of *entrepreneur* who changes the existing economic order by introducing innovations. Diversity that leads to economic change and technological innovations are the origins of variety. Heroic entrepreneurs move the economy from one state of stability to the next, whereby the principle of "creative destruction" comes into play. To achieve this, the stagnation of balanced states must first be dissolved before the newly created spaces can be filled with innovations. In this sense companies do not develop on tracks of linear legality, but are driven by erratic fluctuations.

In terms of leadership, the *intrapreneur* is thought to be a secret recipe for the revitalization of large companies. It becomes the central task of management to motivate the employees to reach their goals. Ideally, in doing so, the charisma of the intrapreneurs should jump from the leaders to the employees. Intrapreneurs thus function as catalysts for the transformation of companies.

Interpreneurs no longer limit their radius of action to the internal organization alone. They recognize that networked companies only have thin, porous, and permeable boundaries to the outside world and direct their company actions accordingly. In networked companies, the relationships to suppliers, customers, authorities, and the public are no longer monopolized in a certain area of the company. This permits potentially every employee to take advantage of these permeable environmental relationships. The task of the interpreneur must be to promote and stimulate the relationships with the environment and thereby release processes of organizational learning—horizontally as well as vertically. This is more than a balance between stability and flexibility. A quantitative jump between these two mechanisms occurs. This explains how companies can break into smaller units and develop into powerful actors through networking and at the same time they are able to use external chaos without losing their flexibility.

The Schumpeter Principle of Creative Destruction

Normally the term entrepreneur refers to the owner or manager of a company. Schumpeter believes that entrepreneur is a sort of mark of nobility, only suitable for innovative personalities. Whoever supervises the smooth management of firms is, according to Schumpeter, not entitled to be classified as an entrepreneur. In his theory of economic development (1934) he identifies the manager with the active person who realizes ideas. He stirs up the economic balance by influencing the needs of the consumers, like an energy source within the economic system. The motivation of such a defined entrepreneur cannot be compared to the ideal of *Homo Oeconomicus*, who originally was the idol brought about by the classic economic theory fixated on individual benefits. According to Schumpeter, innovations are explainable through a different kind of rationalism. Companies are restless in their search for new combinations and destroy previous states of equilibrium.

The representatives of the classic economic theory explained the market as an interplay of supply and demand in which the competitors mutually underbid in price. The price mechanism causes a balance of supply and demand and causes a stable and lasting price to set in that is usually slightly above manufacturing costs. If this price is reached then a state of equilibrium sets in. Value and price of goods are greatly dependent on the use that a consumer expects from them. Industrialists and consumers orient themselves on the maximization of benefits. Schumpeter thought that this picture of a market based on complete information and tailored to the pure maximizing of its benefits is more wishful thinking than factual. The real market is never stationary, but can also never be stable, since the economic subjects operating in the market are implicitly separated from one another to gain competitive advantages. The competition of products and production processes are more important than price competition. This idea is shown in Figure 5.1.

According to Schumpeter (1942), competition was especially made up of the process of creative destruction, in which newer and qualitatively better production processes and products pushed aside the old processes and products. According to this idea, the history of capitalism is the history of technical revolution. In this way, for example, the car destroyed the horse carriage and the computer destroyed the typewriter. The examination of technical renewals, and thus of innovations, played an important role in Schumpeter's thinking insofar as he was trying to find the forces that lift the economic balance from its hinges. As the driving force of every

FIGURE 5.1. Entrepreneurship and Creative Destruction

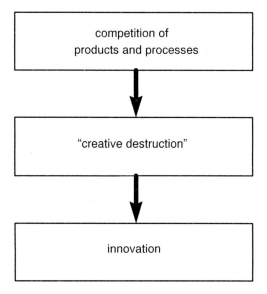

economic change, Schumpeter sees a type of entrepreneur who, in the search for innovations, creatively destroys or changes existing economic connections.

By innovations, Schumpeter meant any possible change in the method of supplying goods: the invention and development of new products, or the improvement of products, as well as the introduction and development of new production methods. It is important that not every new idea or invention represents an innovation. Moreover, it is part of an innovation to have a new idea actually get onto the market. Only then is an innovation seen as useful and profitable, if it is distributed widely enough.

Another characteristic of an innovation is that it is erratic. Innovations are almost never due to consumers changing their tastes or needs, but rather because creative entrepreneurs invent needs and substantially influence the tastes of the consumers.

Management in Large Firms

According to Schumpeter, the creative entrepreneur is the motor that keeps the technical advance in gear and thus increases general prosperity. At the same time, however, the entrepreneur pushes the less innovative competitors along the process of creative destruction into bankruptcy. Historically seen, this is how large companies developed. In large companies a fighting initiative is required less often. Detailed planning processes, statistical controlling instruments, and organized forms are all necessary. In large companies the danger exists that business-minded personalities will become uninspired employees who operate according to clearly stated organizational routines.

Today's economy is formed by large companies that are led by employees rather than by creative entrepreneurs. If entrepreneurs are successful, their companies almost inevitably change to organizations of hierarchy. From modest beginnings, large Japanese firms such as Sony or Honda often develop in the second or third management generation into bureaucratically led firms in which early dynamic action gives way to central decision structures. Companies thus undermine their own success. In such a state of development, leader personalities that can point to future action options may function as *intrapreneurs*.

Intrapreneurs need to give their organizations cultural identity and future-oriented vision. Intrapreneurship puts the emphasis on diffusion of economic spirit in wide areas of the company. According to Shimizu (1991), the goal is to work against bureaucratic structures in large companies. The theories of intrapreneurship state that visionary individuals can function as catalysts for the transformation of companies (Pinchot, 1986). Leading personalities are able to balance out and integrate areas of tension within the company in order to ultimately achieve change. Organizational change guarantees increased productivity and efficiency within companies (see Figure 5.2).

The different ideas about intrapreneurship emphasize the charismatic character of successful leader personalities. Their charisma is supposed to motivate employees and convey wisdom. Max Weber (1993) describes charisma as a legitimate power of leadership. The charismatic character of leadership contains both rational and traditional elements. The special radiation of a charismatic personality can make the existing leadership appear legitimate even if the strategy (rationality) and the culture (tradition) of a company call for different leadership. Max Weber emphasizes the special revolutionary character of charisma. In its genuine form it can explode rationality and tradition. Charismatic personalities, according to Weber, gather supporters around themselves.

FIGURE 5.2. Changing Power of Intrapreneurs

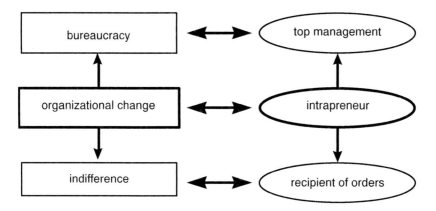

Charisma in companies is connected to a certain quality that enables leaders to mobilize action potential in organizations. Intrapreneurship thus follows an essential aspect of change management. Charismatic leaders should, however, have characteristics beyond genuine charisma. Leadership should be supplemented with rational and traditional elements in order to really be efficient. In contrast to Max Weber, the theories of intrapreneurship do not isolate charisma as the so-called revolutionary element of leadership, but supplement it by historic perspectives of strategies and cultures (Nadler and Tushman, 1990).

The usable ideas of intrapreneurship further include the role of middle managers (Fulup, 1991). Managers on the leadership level contribute incrementally to innovation and thus act similar to entrepreneurs. The modern "heroes" in the organizational developmental process are not just the top managers anymore, but rather the employees who are trusted with leadership tasks at the base of the company. Thus intrapreneurship ideally shows up daily in R&D, production, sales, and administration. In this sense Nodoushani (1991) also talks about the end of the management society. Or in other words: every organizational member has the opportunity to participate in the management of the firm.

Interpreneurship As a Paradigm for the Twenty-First Century

Why do Japanese entrepreneurs face so many obstacles when it comes to trying out new ideas? Japan is home to world-class multinationals, and the world's biggest stash of savings. Yet it fails at freeing up those resources for promising start-ups, providing incentives for managers to challenge old ideas, or marshaling Japan's considerable research and development spending into breakthrough products and industries. If the future belongs to economies driven by innovation and knowledge, where does that leave Japan?

The problem runs deeper than the banking crisis that has grabbed headlines of late. If Japan is to regain its edge, its entire economic model will need rethinking. For decades, well-trained bureaucrats have funneled capital to export-oriented industries. It worked brilliantly during Japan's postwar catch-up phase. Not so in this decade—since 1992.

Fostering start-ups in leading-edge businesses has only recently become a priority in Japan. There is precious little tracking or promotion of the entrepreneurial sector. Only now, with high technology fueling impressive growth in the United States, are Japanese policymakers and economists starting to take notice. The MITI, which for years coddled the manufacturing sector, has begun to draft new policies in hopes of spurring the creation of trans-*keiretsu* ventures in the high-tech sector.

We should discuss and propose a new, hypothetical type of entrepreneur in Japan: the *interpreneur*. The interpreneur overcomes the mentioned problems and develops a new worldview that is far beyond the more traditional concepts of entrepreneurship and intrapreneurship. The connection of corporations in strategic networks calls for a redefinition of the term corporations. Corporations that follow a cooperative strategy contradict the principle of creative destruction because they altruistically develop along a mutual axis of development with other enterprises. Environments are not being destroyed, but instead are generated purposely and are goal oriented in an interactive atmosphere of mutual trust. Also the pure inside perspective of a charismatic leader who develops visions of future goals and concepts for his or her company only is no longer up to date. Companies have too many points of interaction with their environment so it is necessary to pay attention to these interactions. Entrepreneurs in the age of strategic networks must still have the creative touch of a Schumpeter entrepreneur and the charismatic personality to produce innovations and to motivate employees. Today, however, these traits alone are no longer sufficient. They must be aware of their own interest as well as that of their company to be integrated into a strategic network and they must develop action alternatives accordingly. Managers of this new caliber are referred to as *interpreneurs*, and the underlying management principle is referred to as *interpreneurship*. The essential characteristics of a postmodern interpreneurship can be developed from those of the entrepreneur as well as the intrapreneur (see Figure 5.3).

According to Schumpeter (1942), companies are considered open toward their environment, from which they receive their important resources. The entrepreneur forms the corporate structures in reaction to the laws of the environment. The environment is

FIGURE 5.3. The Interpreneur in Comparison to Entrepreneur and Intrapreneur

	Entrepreneur	Intrapreneur	Interpreneur
system	open	closed	permeable
evolution	Darwinistic	egocentric	(weak) altruistic
innovation	technical	processal	social
learning	individual	organization	network

interpreted for one's own interests, so that the external relationships are usually shaped antagonistically and by short, changing manipulations. The entrepreneur sees the environment as a source of uncertainty and creates innovations from environmental nourishment and endangerment under pressure.

Intrapreneurship, on the other hand, is based on the idea of a closed system. Leaders act within the tight boundaries of their organization. They try to optimize the interaction of the organizational members by channeling and integrating opinions, abilities, and habits. Closed and self-centered organizations are headed by leaders who lack the connecting link to the environment.

A special type of entrepreneur is unnerved if an enterprise is acting in a turbulent environment. It must be the goal to establish a systemic relation between the enterprises and their environments. Shareff (1991) states that it is essential for an entrepreneur to establish a good partnership with the environment to secure the ability to compete in the long run. The so-called "ecovisions" create exchange relations between enterprises and their environments. In this sense, the boundaries between the systems are neither open nor closed, but permeable instead. Suggestions as well as rejections from the environment can easily reach the enterprise and its organization members. Consequently, permeable organizations can react with more flexibility than in the case of an open organization.

Schumpeter admired Darwin and states that Darwin's evolutionary theory is important for understanding economic changes and shows the destructive role of the entrepreneur. The most important task of the entrepreneur is the destruction of the given order, because success can make resistance turn into change. The will to succeed is the most important driving force of the capitalistic order. Individual success automatically leads to competition of old-fashioned companies and their connected existences. Only the strongest companies have a chance for survival. The idea of creative destruction is based on Darwin's principle of selection. Companies that do not reach their adaptive goals might be eliminated. Development and change in a company occurs in a sequence of variation, selection, and retention. The evolutionary idea in Schumpeter's view of an entrepreneur is thus definitely formed by Darwinism.

Intrapreneurs, on the other hand, trust their company's growth potential. They try to form the organizational process in an exemplary and charismatic way in order to catapult their organization into the highest possible position. The evolutionary process is especially geared toward internal growth and is thus egocentric. Large companies are usually so busy with themselves that influences from the outside—such as customer demands or competition—are seen as bothersome.

In the case of interpreneurship, companies move within an altruistic relationship with their environments. They rarely develop as single units through adaptation to the hostile-perceived environment or through the concentration on internal growth potentials. Rather they evolve together with their environment. They exchange knowledge resources with companies integrated in a strategic network. By doing so, however, they sometimes sacrifice evolutionary speed in the short term because they strengthen the competitiveness of the environment. But they receive indirect long-run rewards that compensate for the immediate sacrifice.

Schumpeter's (1934) entrepreneur revitalizes organizations primarily through technical innovations. Technical innovations create market competitiveness and secure the survival of the firm. Schumpeter attributed the importance of technical innovations to the fact that the technical achievements of the first industrial revolution fundamentally changed the sociocultural mind of humankind.

Intrapreneurship theorems emphasize the processal transformation of firms. Intrapreneurship can be conceived of not only as technical innovation; it also includes innovation in organizational structures and processes. Organizations are shaped by their leaders and management visions are good opportunities for a transformation of the firm. Hence, one could talk about processal innovations by leaders who are smoothly changing the behavior of their employees and of their organization as a whole.

Due to binding into a strategic network, interpreneurs have the opportunity to initiate social innovations in their environment. Social innovations include the renewal of basic models of social interaction. Strategic networks cannot be managed by fencing them off from hostile-perceived environments. Rather they must be developed and shaped in an atmosphere of mutual trust. Interpreneurship demands a positional shift of the dominating paradigm of capitalism. Interpreneurship is and cannot be separated by society. Interpreneurs rather can and must give contributions to social advances.

The learning behavior in the model of the Schumpeter entrepreneur is essentially anchored within the company. Entrepreneurs are heroic exceptions who have specific abilities that separate them from "normal" individuals. They direct the development of their company through individual learning abilities and with the help of their accumulated knowledge. They are active in realizing their ideas. Usually the experiences from previous successes or failures are not shared with the other organizational members. Learning remains limited to single individuals such as the entrepreneurs.

According to the view of intrapreneurship, leaders promote the learning abilities of all organizational members and the entire organization. They set goals for the organizational members and support their efforts to reach the goals. Organizations learn in a way that differs from the sum of the individual learning processes. Individual knowledge is ideally made accessible to all organizational members and is further developed in the sense of a collective socialization process. The focus of learning is pushed onto organizations.

By entering a strategic network, the learning focus is shifted onto the companies that are bound into the network. Permeable organizational boundaries allow the exchange of knowledge and its utilization of new knowledge. The learning focus is clearly on the network in which vertical learning sequences within the company are linked to horizontal ones. Interfirm learning is anchored in the daily routine of work life and is constantly demanded by the interpreneur. He demands this from the employees of the original company as well as from the cooperative partners.

There is a new type of entrepreneur in Japan who is different from Schumpeter's legacy and from the leadership theorems. The interpreneur develops abilities within small businesses. Japanese small businesses are increasingly playing a large role in shaping the Japanese economic structure. The world of Japanese business, according to conventional thinking, only consists of huge *keiretsu* firms, whereas start-ups by entrepreneurs are seldom recognized. Due to the creative visions of entrepreneurial individuals, start-ups are a major source of employment and of economic growth. Though the number of newly established firms is increasing since the first half of the 1990s, there are still not many small venture firms. The successful firms are pursuing a network strategy. They build up trans-*keiretsu* networks for developing and marketing new technologies. The following illustrates the example of Suzuki Sogyo, a Japanese venture firm that is managing its businesses within a strategic network.

Although Suzuki Sogyo was established as a trading firm, it was reborn as a high-technology firm in the 1980s. At present, its main business is "printing on the curved surface" and the "gel" business. The printing technology is used for car interiors, whereas the gel is a kind of silicone used for sport shoes. The firm employs 200 persons and has a sales figure of about 30 billion yen per year.

Both technologies have been developed in cooperation with other Japanese firms of approximately the same size. Mr. Nakanishi, the president of the company, initiated contacts with start-up firms, which also have had interests in developing those business lines. During the phase of common R&D, there was almost no organizational boundary between Suzuki Sogyo and its partners. The network alliances existed only temporarily and were dissolved after the products were developed.

Today, Suzuki Sogyo continuously changes its network partners in order to seek new business opportunities. One instrument of partner search and partner selection is the *igyoushu koryu*, networks of small businesses sponsored by local authorities. Mr. Nakanishi also analyzes all kinds of social information around him to be provided with tips on new technologies and potential network partners. Within the company, Mr. Nakanishi actively transmits the knowledge that he and his employees grafted from the network partners. He promotes internal and external employee transfers to enhance vertical and horizontal learning. Mr. Nakanishi opposes formal cooperation, whether involving individuals or firms. Organizational learning is perceived and lived as a self-organizing process.

Strategic networks are an entrepreneurial trial to organize an uncertain environment and structure it tighter. In other words, it is about building organizational elements into stable and turbulent environmental relationships to increase stability. Similarly, Johannisson (1987) holds the opinion that entrepreneurs have to be both anarchists and organizers in a network setting. The ideal interpreneur, as conceptually developed in this chapter, has destructive elements that are in accordance with organizational goals. The interpreneur believes that environmental relationships cannot be navigated, but must be developed along a planned evolution.

Chapter 6

Final Remarks

This book makes an appeal for companies to voluntarily relinquish extensive planning and direction and to become open to the concept of a network. The example of strategic networks in Japan shows that if companies refrain from total control they can achieve new knowledge potentials and thus increase their ability to compete. Question marks would often be more suitable at the end of the recipes for shaping new organizations than the exclamation marks that are popular with many managers. Uncertainty and unsureness, which are ever present in strategic networks, are also suitable for the new type of manager, the interpreneur. General statements as well as general advice about companies become increasingly difficult. This is due to the delicate nature of interfirm links and the greater importance that flexibility plays rather than stability.

Competition and cooperation supplement each other and are essential for human beings. Competition can support cooperation and on the flip side, cooperation can stimulate competition. The balance between the two, not the forceful suppression of the poles, is important to see what forces can mobilize the basic economic order. The previous order that is based on antagonistic competition is, according to Popper (1945), mostly a closed order. In bureaucratic companies that stand alone among a number of competitors, an anachronism sets in. This is a regression to an old-fashioned, historical, mythological, magical society. Popper equates "closed" with "magical" since he can see a tendency in this societal form to mystify and glorify existing models. Closed societies or organizations are so busy doing what they learned to do that they neglect to ask background questions about old action models.

The closed organization that is usually busy with itself and is shielded from the environment of surrounding networks will not disappear quickly. However, this type of organization is currently undergoing dramatic changes. Popper (1945) even predicts that structures that are linked to bureaucracy, dogmatism, and antagonism will die in the long run. He states that they are inefficient and their management is irrational. They will be able to develop only with much effort, at great cost, and slowly.

The phenomenal growth of Japan in the 1970s and 1980s was one of the important factors in promoting strategic networks. The collapse of the "bubble economy" in 1992 and the Asian economic crisis of 1997 onward revealed stark cracks in Japan's once imposing facade. While the old mandarins, like the once-exalted Finance Ministry, have been discredited, no new respected institutions have risen to take their place. The opposition parties, divided by both lack of ideas and personal squabbles, have been ineffective so far. However, as Katz (1998) puts it, Japan is a great nation trapped in the straitjacket of obsolete institutions. Those institutions will eventually break and Japan will thrive once it makes the necessary changes. Japan's history shows that the country often had fast rises and hard falls, but it always rose again. Japan's modern ascent began with the sweeping nineteenth-century reforms of the Meiji Restoration. The goal was to catch up to the industrialized West. Military defeat in 1945 brought a hard fall, but then came another takeoff—and one of the most dramatic half-centuries of progress the world has ever seen.

Now Japan is rising again. This time, it has only to catch up with itself. The Meiji Restoration was a paradigm of sweeping change, and it was total in its impact, encompassing the politics, economy, and society of Japan. Now we have come to a similar era in history. Although some Japanese firms are still enjoying record profits, an increasing number of firms are underperforming. The financial sector, in particular, is collapsing. In addition, domestic prices are too high, the government spends too much, and the system that built an export powerhouse is eroding. The continued Japanese recession has led many observers to conclude that Japan is now facing an extended era of near-zero economic growth. Prime Minister Obuchi's action plan is the so-called Big Bang package of measures that by the turn of the millennium will eliminate much of the red tape restricting Japan's financial sector. This will lower brokerage commissions, allow banks and securities companies into one another's businesses, and break down barriers to foreign competition. Japan's *keiretsu* are now going through a process of reorientation and remanagement to develop new and innovative forms of interfirm relations that will be able to withstand and overcome the recent economic turmoil.

Thus the network paradigm is at a critical crossroads in Japan. Or, as Tezuka (1997) states, the success of networks may be the source of recent economic failure. Drastic changes in the internal and global economic conditions may force a far-reaching transformation of interfirm links, largely eroding traditional *keiretsu*. It may be incorrect, however, to place blame for problems in Japan on the *keiretsu* since there are a number of external factors—in particular the link with the surrounding Asian economies and therefore the impact of the Asian economic crisis. Now new types of strategic networks have to lead the country through yet another of its masterful transformations.

The network paradigm is alive, though it is no longer an imperative. The network relationship turns out to be an element of a broader and more complex relationship nexus. Japanese-style strategic networks are becoming a part of an interfirm system forming an international, and particularly Asian basis.

We live in a world of uncertainty. Whatever we do is only a trial, a rough draft that can very well be a mistake. An objective certainty about the existence of truth can actually never be achieved, for there are no criteria for truth and there is no guarantee for it either. Whoever wants to instill a network culture must first make sure that no dogmatic thoughts are anchored within the organization. The perspective of a network culture allows us to accept the uncontrollability and uncertainty of economic actions. Furthermore it is a perspective that allows us to encourage new designs and ideas. These are desirable, not because they are new, but because the economy has changed and will continue to change. New economic demands open up new horizons. Strategic networks are an option with a future.

References

Abegglen, J.C. and Stalk Jr, G. (1987). *Kaisha: The Japanese Corporation*, Tokyo: Charles E. Tuttle.

Abo, T. (1995). A Comparison of Japanese Hybrid Factories in the U.S., Europe, and Asia. *Management International Review*, 35, Special Issue 1995/1, pp. 79-93.

Aburdene, P. (1999). *Self-Organization: The Business Megatrend of the 21st Century*, New York: Simon & Schuster.

Achrol, R.S. (1997). Changes in the Theory of Interorganizational Relations in Marketing: Toward a Network Paradigm. *Journal of the Academy of Marketing Science*, 25(1), pp. 56-71.

Ackoff, R.L. (1993). Corporate Peristroika. In Halal, W.E., Geranmayeh, A., and Pourdehnad, J. (Eds.), *Internal Markets*, New York: John Wiley & Sons, pp. 15-16.

Adams, R.S. (1991). Concluding Observations: The Evolution of Evolutionary Theory and Mechanisms. *Cultural Dynamics*, 2, pp. 229-238.

Aldrich, H.E. and Whetten, D.A. (1981). Organization-sets, Action-sets, and Networks: Making the Most of Simplicity. In Nystrom, P.C. and Starbuck, W.H. (Eds.), *Handbook of Organizational Design*, Vol. 1, Oxford: Oxford University Press, pp. 385-400.

Alevsson, A. and Berg, P.O. (1992). *Corporate Culture and Organizational Symbolism*, Berlin: de Gruyter.

Alic, K.A., Branscomb, H., Brooks, H., Carter, A., and Epstein, G.L. (1992). *Beyond Spinoff*, Boston: Harvard Business School Press.

Anderson, J.C., Hakansson, H., and Johanson, J. (1994). Dyadic Business Relationships Within a Business Network Context. *Journal of Marketing Research*, 29 (February), pp. 18-34.

Anderson, P. and Yoshimura, N. (1997). *Inside the Kaisha*, Boston: Harvard Business School Press.

Aoki, M. (1984). *The Cooperative Game Theory of the Firm*, Oxford: Oxford University Press.

Aoki, M. (1988). *Information, Incentives, and Bargaining in the Japanese Economy*, Cambridge: Cambridge University Press.

Argyris, C. and Schön, D.A. (1978). *Organizational Learning: A Theory of Action Perspective*, Reading, MA: Addison-Wesley.

Ashby, W.R. (1958). Requisite Variety and Its Implications for the Control of Complex Systems. *Cybernetica*, 1, pp. 83-96.

Axelrod, R. (1984). *The Evolution of Cooperation*, New York: Basic Books.

Axelsson, B. and Easton, G. (Eds.) (1992). *Industrial Networks: A New View of Reality*, London: Routledge.

Bachnik, J. (1992). Kejime: Defining a Shifting Self in Multiple Organizational Modes. In Rosenberger, N.R. (Ed.), *Japanese Sense of Self,* Cambridge, England: Cambridge University Press, pp. 152-172.

Badaracco, J.L. (1991). *The Knowledge Link: How Firms Compete Through Strategic Alliances,* Boston: Harvard Business School Press.

Baker, W.E. (1990). Market Networks and Corporate Behavior. *American Journal of Sociology,* 96(3), pp. 589-625.

Baker, W.E. (1992). The Network Organization in Theory and Practice. In Nohria, N. and Eccles, R.G. (Eds.), *Networks and Organizations: Structure, Form and Action,* Boston: Harvard University Press, pp. 397-429.

Banerji, K. and Sambharya, R.B. (1996). Vertical *Keiretsu* and International Market Entry: The Case of the Japanese Automobile Ancillary Industry. *Journal of International Business Studies,* First Quarter 1996, pp. 89-113.

Barlett, C.A. and Ghoshal, S. (1987). Managing Across Borders: New Strategic Requirements. *Sloan Management Review,* Summer 1987, pp. 37-47.

Bartu, F. (1992). *The Ugly Japanese: Nippon's Economic Empire in Asia,* Tokyo: Yenbooks.

Beck, J.C. and Hansen, T. (1993). Lessons from Japan: American and Japanese Strategies and Goals in the 1990s. *The International Executive,* 35(5), pp. 445-460.

Beckhard, R. and Harris, R.T. (1978). *Organizational Transition—Managing Complex Change,* Reading, MA: Addison-Wesley.

Berque, A. (1992). Identification of the Self in Relation to the Environment. In Rosenberger, N.R. (Ed.), *Japanese Sense of Self,* Cambridge, England: Cambridge University Press, pp. 93-104.

Bygrave, W.D. (1988). The Structure of the Investment Networks of Venture Capital Firms. *Journal of Business Venturing,* 3, pp. 137-157.

Byrne, J.A. (1993). The Virtual Cooperation. *International Business Week,* 8(2), pp. 36-41.

Calenbuhr, V. (1996). What Can We Learn from Biological Networks? In Richter, F.-J. (Ed.), *The Dynamics of Japanese Organizations,* London: Routledge, pp. 72-91.

Cameren, C. (1991): Does Strategy Research Need Game Theory? *Strategic Management Journal,* 3, pp. 137-152.

Carlsson, B. and Stankiewicz, R. (1991). On the Nature, Function, and Composition of Technological Systems. *Journal of Evolutionary Economics,* 1, pp. 93-118.

Casson, M. (1990). *Enterprise and Competitiveness—A Systems View of International Business,* Oxford, England: Oxford University Press.

Celeste, R.F. (1996). Strategic Alliances for Innovation: Emerging Models of Technology-Based Twenty-First Century Economic Development. *Economic Development Review,* Winter, pp. 4-8.

Chen, E. and Hamilton, G.G. (1991). Introduction: Business Networks and Economic Development. In Hamilton, G. (Ed.), *Business Networks and Economic Development in East and Southeast Asia,* Hong Kong: Centre of Asian Studies, University of Hongkong, pp. 3-10.

Chikudate, N. (1995). Communication Network Liaisons As Cultural Interpreters for Organizational Adaptation in Japan-Europe Business Environments. *Management International Review*, Special Issue 1995/2, pp. 27-38.

Chikudate, N. (1996). Communication Through On-Line Database Systems: A Strategy for Monitoring Corporate Environments. In Richter, F.-J. (Ed.), *The Dynamics of Japanese Organizations*, London: Routledge, pp. 178-188.

Chisholm, R.F. (1997). *Developing Network Organizations: Learning from Practice and Theory*, Reading, MA: Addison-Wesley.

Christensen, P. (1991). Driving Forces, Increasing Returns, and Ecological Sustainability. In Constanza, R. (Ed.), *Ecological Economics: The Science and Management of Sustainability*, New York: Columbia University Press, pp. 74-87.

Christopher, M. (1993). Logistics and Competitive Strategy. *European Management Journal*, 2, pp. 258-261.

Clark, C.W. (1991). Economic Biases Against Sustainable Development. In Constanza, R. (Ed.), *Ecological Economics: The Science and Management of Sustainability*, New York: Columbia University Press, pp. 319-330.

Cole, R.E. and Yakushiji, T. (1984). *The American and Japanese Autoparts Industries in Transition*, Ann Arbor, MI: Center for Japanese Studies Press.

Colombo, M.G. (Ed.) (1998). *Changing Boundaries of the Firm: Explaining Evolving Inter-Firm Relations*, London: Routledge.

Cook, K.S. and Emerson, R.M. (1984). Exchange Networks and the Analysis of Complex Organizations. In Bacharach, S.B. and Lawler, E.J. (Eds.), *Research in the Sociology of Organizations*, (3), Greenwich, CT: JAI, pp. 1-30.

Cusumano, M.A. (1991). *Japan's Software Factories: A Challenge to U.S. Management*. Oxford, England: Oxford University Press, 1991.

Cusumano, M.A. and Takeishi, A. (1991). Supplier Relations and Management: A Survey of Japanese, Japanese-Transplant, and U.S. Autoplants. *Strategic Management Journal*, 12, pp. 563-588.

Cutts, R.L. (1992). Capitalism in Japan: Cartels and *Keiretsu, Harvard Business Review*, 70, pp. 48-55.

Czarniawska-Joerges (1992). *Exploring Complex Organizations: A Cultural Perspective*, Newbury Park, CA: Sage.

Czinkota, M.R. and Woronoff, J. (1991). *Unlocking Japan's Markets: Seizing Marketing and Distribution Opportunities in Today's Japan*, Chicago: Probus Publishing.

Daft, R.L. and Huber, G.B. (1987). How Organizations Learn: A Communication Framework. In Ditomasu, N. and Bacharach, S. (Eds.). *Research in the Sociology of Organizations*, Vol. 5, Greenwich, CT: JAI, pp. 1-36.

Davis, S. and Meyer, C. (1997). *Blur: The Speed of Change in the Connected Economy*, Reading, MA: Addison-Wesley.

Davidow, W.H. and Malone, M.S. (1992). *The Virtual Corporation: Structuring and Revitalizing the Corporation for the 21st Century*, New York: Harper Business.

de Geus, Arie (1997). *The Living Company*, Boston: Harvard Business School Press.

DeBresson, C. and Amesse, F. (1991). Networks of Innovators: A Review and Introduction to the Issue. *Research Policy*, 20(5), pp. 363-380.

Demes, H. (1992). The Japanese Production Mode As Model for the 21st Century. In Tokunaga, S., Altmann, N., and Demes, H. (Eds.), *New Impacts on Industrial Relations*, Munich, Germany: Iudicium, pp. 469-488.

Deyer, J.H. (1995). Specialized Networks As a Source of Competitive Advantage: Evidence from the Auto Industry. *Strategic Management Journal*, 17, pp. 271-291.

Deyer, J.H. (1996). How Chrysler Created an American *Keiretsu*. *Harvard Business Review*, 74(4), July/August, pp. 42-56.

Dirks, D. (1994). Organizational Development in Japanese Overseas Subsidiaries. In Campbell, N. and Burton, F. (Eds.), *Japanese Multinationals. Strategies and Management in the Global Kaisha*, London: Routledge, pp. 252-273.

Dirks, D. (1995). The Quest for Organizational Competence: Japanese Management Abroad. *Management International Review*, Special Issue 1995/2, pp. 75-90.

Doi, T. (1986). *The Anatomy of Self. The Individual versus Society*, Tokyo: Kondansha International.

Dore, R. (1994). Japanese Capitalism, Anglo-Saxon Capitalism: How Will the Darwinian Contest Turn Out? In Campbell, N. and Burton, F. (Eds.), *Japanese Multinationals: Strategies and Management in the Global Kaisha*, London: Routledge, pp. 9-28.

Dosi, G. (1988). Sources, Procedures, and Microeconomic Effects of Innovation. *Journal of Economic Literature*, 26, pp. 1120-1171.

Drucker, P. (1954). *The Practice of Management*, New York: HarperBusiness.

Drucker, P. (1980). *Managing in Turbulent Times*, New York: Harper and Row.

Drucker, P. (1988). Management and the World's Work, *Harvard Business Review*, 66, September/October, pp. 65-76.

Drucker, P. (1993). *The Post-Capitalist Society*, New York: Harper Business.

Dunning, J.H. (1997). *Alliance Capitalism and Global Business*, London: Routledge.

Dyer, J. (1996). Does Governance Matter? *Keiretsu* Alliances an Asset Specificity As Sources of Japanese Competitive Advantage, *Strategic Management Journal*, 7, pp. 1071-1088.

Eads, G.C. (1990). Geography Is not Destiny: The Changing Character of Competitive Advantage in Automobiles. In Heiduk, H. and Yamamura, K. (Eds.), *Technological Competition and Interdependence*, Seattle/London: University of Washington Press, pp. 212-232.

Eccles, R.G. and Crane, D.B. (1987). Managing Through Networks in Investment Banking. *California Management Review*, 30, pp. 176-194.

Engwall, L. and Johanson, J. (1990). Banks in Industrial Networks. *Scandinavian Journal of Management*, 6(3), pp. 231-244.

Emerson, R.M. (1981). Social Exchange Theory. In Rosenberg, M. and Turner, R.H. (Eds.), *Social Psychology: Sociological Perspectives*, New York: Academic Press, pp. 30-65.

Eisenhardt, K. (1989). Agency-Theory: An Assessment Review. *Academy of Management Review*, 14(1) pp. 57-74.

Evan, W. (1965). The Organization Set: Toward a Theory of Interorganizational Relations. *Management Science*, 11, pp. 217-230.

Fallows, J. (1994). *Looking at the Sun: The Rise of the New East Asian Economic and Political System*, New York: Pantheon Books.

Fedor, K.J. and Werther Jr. W.B. (1995). Making Sense of Cultural Factors in International Alliances. *Organizational Dynamics*, Spring 1995, pp. 33-48.

Ferguson, C.H. (1990). Computers and the Coming of the U.S. *Keiretsu. Harvard Business Review*, July-August, pp. 55-70.

Ford, I.D., Gadde, L.E., Hakansson, H., and Ford, D. (Eds.) (1998). *Managing Business Relationships*, New York: John Wiley & Sons.

Fornengo, G. (1988). Manufacturing Networks: Telematics in the Automotive Industry. In Antonelli, C. (Ed.), *New Information Technology and Industrial Change*, Dodrecht, Netherlands: Kluwer, pp. 33-56.

Forrester, J.W. (1958). Industrial Dynamics: A Major Breakthrough for Decision Makers. *Harvard Business Review*, 4, pp. 37-66.

Foss, N.J. (Ed.) (1997). *Economic Organization, Capabilities and Co-Ordination Essays in Honour of G.B. Richardson*, London: Routledge.

Fransman, M. (1990). *The Market and Beyond: Cooperation and Competition in Information Technology Development in the Japanese System*, New York: Cambridge University Press.

Fruin, M.W. (1992). *The Japanese Enterprise System.* Oxford, England: Clarendon Press.

Fruin, M.W. (1997). *Knowledge Works: Managing Intellectual Capital at Toshiba*, Oxford, England: Oxford University Press.

Fruin, M.W. (Ed.) (1998). *Networks and Markets: Pacific Rim Strategies*, Oxford, England: Oxford University Press.

Fulup, L. (1991). Middle Managers: Victims or Vanguards of the Entrepreneurial Movement? *Journal of Management Studies*, 28(1), pp. 25-35.

Fukuyama, F. (1995). *Trust*, New York: The Free Press.

Furukawa (1985). Igyoushu koyru no shorai (The Future of igyoushu koyru), *Shoukou kinyu*, 35(6), pp. 14-23.

Gadamer, H.G. (1977). *Philosophical Hermeneutics*, Berkeley, CA: University of California Press.

Gadde, L.E. and Mattson, I.G. (1987). Stability and Change in Network Relationships. *International Journal of Research in Marketing*, 4(1), pp. 29-41.

Galbraith, J.R. (1982). Designing the Innovating Organization. *Organizational Dynamics*, Winter, pp. 5-25.

Garvin, D. (1993). Building a Learning Organization. *Harvard Business Review*, 71, July-August, pp. 78-91.

Gemünden, H.G., Ritter, T., and Heydebreck, P. (1996). Network Configuration and Innovation Success: An Empirical Analysis in German High-Tech Industries. *International Research in Marketing*, 13, pp. 449-462.

Gemünden, H.G., Ritter, T., and Walter, A. (Eds.) (1998). *Relationships and Networks in International Markets*, New York: Elsevier.

Gerlach, M.L. (1992). *Alliance Capitalism. The Social Organization of Japanese Business*, Berkeley, CA: University of California Press.

Gilroy, B.M. (1993). *Networking in Multinational Enterprises*, Columbia, SC: University of South Carolina Press.

Goldman, A. (1994). *Doing Business with the Japanese: A Guide to Successful Communication, Management, and Diplomacy*, Albany, NY: State University of New York Press.

Granovetter, M. (1973). The Strength of Weak Ties. *American Journal of Sociology*, 6, pp. 1360-1380.

Grant, R.M. (1991). The Resource-Based Theory of Competitive Advantage. Implications for Strategy Formulation. *California Management Review*, 33 (Spring), pp. 114-135.

Grant, R.M. (1996). Prospering in Dynamically-Competitive Environments: Organizational Capability As Knowledge Integration, *Organization Science*, 7(4), pp. 375-387.

Group of Lisbon (1995). *Limits of Competition*, Cambridge, MA: MIT Press.

Gupta, A.K. and Govindarajan, V. (1991). Knowledge Flow and the Structure of Control Within Multinational Corporations. *Academy of Management Review*, 16(4), pp. 768-792.

Hadjikhani, A. and Hakansson, H. (1996). Political Actions in Business Networks: A Swedish Case. *International Journal of Research in Marketing*, 13, pp. 431-447.

Hagedoorn, J. and Schakenraad, J. (1994). The Effect of Strategic Technology Alliances on Company Performance. *Strategic Management Journal*, 15(4), pp. 291-309.

Hakansson, H. (1989). *Corporate Technological Behaviour. Co-operation and Networks*, London: Routledge.

Hakansson, H. and Snehota I. (Eds.) (1995). *Developing Relationships in Business Networks*, London: Routledge.

Haley, G. and Haley, U. (1999). Weaving Opportunities: Overseas Chinese and Overseas Indian Networks in Southeast Asia. In Richter, F.-J. (Ed.), *Business Networks in Asia*, Westport, CT: Quorum (forthcoming).

Hall, I.P. (1998). *Cartels of the Mind: Japan's Intellectual Closed Shop*, New York: Norton.

Hamel, G. (1991). Competition for Competence and Interpartner Learning Within International Strategic Alliances. *Strategic Management Journal*, 12, pp. 83-103.

Hamel, G. and Prahalad, C.K. (1994). *Competing for the Future*, Boston: Harvard Business School Press.

Hamilton, G. (1991). *Business Networks and Economic Development in East and Southeast Asia*, Hong Kong: Centre of Asian Studies, University of Hong Kong.

Hammer, M. and Champy, J. (1993). *Reengineering the Corporation: A Manifesto for Business Revolution*, New York: Harper Business.

Hannan, M.T. and Freeman, J. (1989). *Organizational Ecology*, Cambridge, MA: Harvard University Press.

Hansen, E.L. (1995). Entrepreneurial Networks and New Organization Growth. *Entrepreneurship Theory & Practice*, 19(4), pp. 7-19.

Hedberg, B. (1981). How Organizations Learn and Unlearn. In Nystrom, P. and Starbuch, W.H. (Eds.), *Handbook of Organizational Design*, New York: McGraw-Hill, pp. 3-27.

Hejl, P.M. (1982). Towards a Theory of Social Systems: Self-Organization and Self-Maintenance, Self-Reference and Syn-Reference. In Ulrich, H. and Probst, G.J.B. (Eds.), *Self-Organization and Management of Social Systems*, Berlin, Germany: Springer, pp. 60-78.

Helleloid, D. and Simonin, B. (1994). Organizational Learning and a Firm's Core Competence. In Hamel, G. and Heene, A. (Eds.), *Competence-Based Competition*, Chichester, England: John Wiley & Sons.

Helper, S. and Levine, D.I. (1992). Long-Term Relations and Product-Market Structure. *The Journal of Law, Economics, & Organization*, 3, pp. 561-581.

Henderson, C. (1998). *Asia Falling? Making Sense of the Asian Currency Crises and Its Aftermath*, Singapore: McGraw-Hill.

Henzler, H. and Rall, W. (1986). Facing Up to the Globalization Challenge. *McKinsey Quarterly*, Winter, pp. 52-68.

Hinterhuber, M.H. and Levin, E.M. (1994). Strategic Networks. The Organization of the Future. *Long Range Planning*, 27(3), pp. 43-53.

Hippel, E.V. (1988). *The Sources of Innovation*, New York/Oxford: Oxford University Press.

Hirata, M. and Okumura, A. (1995). Networking and Entrepreneurship in Japan. In Birley, S. and MacMillan, I.C. (Eds.), *International Entrepreneurship*, London: Routledge.

Hiroshi, O. (1991). Intercorporate Relations in Japan. In Hamilton, G. (Ed.), *Business Networks and Economic Development in East and Southeast Asia*, Centre of Asian Studies, University of Hong Kong: Hong Kong. pp. 219-229.

Hofstede, G. (1980). *Culture's Consequences: International Differences in Work-Related Values*, Beverly Hills: Sage.

Hofstede, G. (1991). *Cultures and Organizations: Software of the Mind*, London: McGraw-Hill.

Hollerman, L. (1988). *Japan, Disincorporated: The Economic Liberalization Process*, Stanford, CA: Hoover Institution Press.

Hoshi, T. (1994). The Economic Role of Corporate Grouping and the Main Bank System. In Aoki, M. and Dore, R. (Eds.), *The Japanese Firm: Sources of Competitive Strength*, Oxford, England: Oxford University Press, pp. 284-309.

Hoyt, E. (1991). *The New Japanese. A Complacent People in a Corrupt Society*, London: Robert Hale.

Huntington, S. (1993). The Clash of Civilisations? *Foreign Affairs*, Summer, pp. 22-49.

Inkpen, A. (1996). Creating Knowledge Through Collaboration. *California Management Review*, 39(1), pp. 123-141.

Imai, K. and Itami, H. (1988). *Nettowaku soshikiron (Discourse of Network Organizations)*, Tokyo: Iwanami Shoten.

Imai, M. (1987). *Kaizen: The Key to Japan's Competitive Success*, Random House: New York.

Inzerelli, G. (1990). The Italian Alternative: Flexible Organization and Social Management. *International Studies of Management and Organization*, 20(4): pp. 6-21.

Ishihara, S. (1991). *The Japan That Can Say No: Why Japan Will Be First Among Equals*, New York: Simon & Schuster.

Ishihara, S. (1994). *No to ieru Ajia* (The Asia That Can Say No), Tokyo: Kobunsha.

Itami, H. (1991a). *Gurokaru managemento—chikyu jidai no nihon kigyo (Global Management—The Japanese Firms of the Present)*, Tokyo: NHK Books.

Itami, H. (1991b). *Nihon no kagaku sangyo—naze sekai ni tachi okureta no ka? (The Japanese Chemical Industry—Why Does It Lag Behind Other Industries?)*, Tokyo: NTT Press.

Itami, H. (1994). *Nihon no jodosha sangyo—naze kyo bure-ki ga kakatta no ka? (The Japanese Automotive Industry—Why Did It Suddenly Come to a Stop?)*, Tokyo: NTT Press.

Jackson, T. (1993). *Turning Japanese. The Fight for Industrial Control of the New Europe*, London: HarperCollins.

Jarillo, J.C. (1988). On Strategic Networks. *Strategic Management Journal*, 9(1), pp. 31-41.

Johannisson, B. (1987). Anarchists and Organizers: Entrepreneurs in a Network Perspective. *International Studies of Management and Organization*, 17, pp. 90-127.

Johanson, J. and Mattson, L.G. (1987). Interorganizational Relations in Industrial Markets: A Network Approach Compared with the Transaction Cost Approach. *International Studies of Management & Organization*, 17(1), pp. 34-48.

Johnson, C. (1993). Comparative Capitalism: The Japanese Difference, *California Management Review*, 35(4), pp. 51-67.

Jones, K. and Shill, W.W. (1991). Allying for Advantage. *The McKinsey Quarterly*, 3, 1991, pp. 73-101.

Kagono, T., Nonaka, I., Sakakibara, K., and Okumura, A. (1985). *Strategic vs. Evolutionary Management: A U.S.-Japan Comparison of Strategy and Organization*. Amsterdam: North-Holland.

Kang, M.H. (1997). *Chaebol Then and Now*, London: Curzon Press.

Kanter, R. (1982). *When Giants Learn to Dance*, London: Macmillan.

Kanter, R. (1995). *World Class. Thriving Locally in the Global Economy*, New York: Simon & Schuster.

Katz, R., (1998). *Japan: The System That Soured*, New York: M.E. Sharpe.

Kearns, R.L. (1991). *Zaibatsu America: How Japanese Firms Are Colonizing Vital U.S. Industries*, New York: The Free Press.

Keough, M. and Doman, A. (1992). The CEO As Organization Designer: An Interview with Professor Jay W. Forrester, *The McKinsey Quarterly*, 28(2), 3-30.

Kester, W.C. (1991). *Japanese Takeovers: The Global Contest for Corporate Control*, Boston: Harvard Business School Press.

Kikuchi, T. (1995). *Japanese Distribution Channels*, Binghamton, NY: International Business Press.

Kidd, J.B. (1994). Globalization Through Localization. In Schütte, H. (Ed.), *The Global Competitiveness of the Japanese Firm*, New York: St. Martin's Press, pp. 265-286.

Kikuzawa, K. (1996). Progressive and Degenerative Problemshifts of Organizations: Organizational Evolutionism Based on Critical Rationalism. In Richter, F.-J. (Ed.), *The Dynamics of Japanese Organizations*, London: Routledge, pp. 116-131.

Killing, J. (1988). Understanding Alliances: The Role of Task and Organizational Complexity. In Contractor, F. and Lorange, P. (Eds.), *Cooperative Strategies in International Business*, Lexington, MA: Lexington Books.

Kim, K., Nishiguchi, T., and Lynn, H. (1997). A Comparative Study of Network Systems Among Korean and Japanese Auto-Parts Suppliers. *The Journal of Productivity*, February, pp. 23-39.

Kitaro, N. (1987). *Intuition and Reflection in Self-Consciousness*, Albany, NY: State University of New York Press.

Kogut, B. (1988). A Study of the Life Cycle of Joint Ventures, *Management International Review*, 9, pp. 39-51.

Kotter, J. (1997). *Matsushita Leadership*, New York: The Free Press.

Krugman, P. (1995). *Development, Geography, and Economic Theory*, Denver, CO: Bradford Books.

Kumon, S. and Rosovsky, H. (1992). *The Political Economy of Japan: Cultural and Social Dynamics*, Stanford: Stanford University Press.

Kuwayama, T. (1992). The Reference Other Orientation. In Rosenberger, N.R. (Ed.), *Japanese Sense of Self*, Cambridge, England: Cambridge University Press, pp. 121-151.

Laage-Hellman, J. (1997). *Business Networks in Japan: Supplier-Customer Interaction in Product Development*, London: Routledge.

Larson, A. (1991). Partner Networks: Leveraging External Ties to Improve Entrepreneurial Performance. *Journal of Business Venturing*, 3, pp. 173-188.

Lasserre, P. and Schütte, H. (1995). *Strategies for Asia Pacific*, Macmillan: London.

Lawrence, P.R. and Lorsch, J.W. (1967). *Organization and Environment: Managing Differentiation and Integration*, Boston: Harvard University Press.

Lei, D. and Slocum, J.W. (1991). Global Strategic Alliances: Payoffs and Pitfalls. *Organizational Dynamics*, Winter, pp. 44-63.

Liebeskind, J., Oliver, A., Zucker, L., and Brewer, M. (1996). Social Networks, Learning, Flexibility: Sourcing Scientific Knowledge in New Biotechnology Firms. *Organization Science*, 7(4), pp. 428-443.

Lincoln, J.R. (1982). Intra- (and Inter-) Organizational Networks. In Bacharach, S.B. (Ed.). *Research in the Sociology of Organizations*, Vol. 1, Greenwich, CT: JAI, pp. 1-38.

Lipnack, J. and Stamps, J. (1996). *The Age of the Network: Organizing Principles for the 21st Century*, New York: John Wiley & Sons.

Lorange, P. and Roos, J. (1992). *Strategic Alliances. Formation, Implementation, and Evolution*, Cambridge, MA: Blackwell.

Luhmann, N. (1995). *Social Systems*, Stanford, CA: Stanford University Press.

Luhmann, N. (1998). *Observations on Modernity*, Stanford, CA: Stanford University Press.

Macbeth, D.K. (1996). Partnering in Internationally Competitive Supply Chains: Principles and Operational Management. In Berndt, R. (Ed.), *Global Management*, Berlin, Germany: Springer, pp. 245-261.

Mahoney, J.T. and Pandian, J.R. (1992). The Resource-Based View Within the Conversation of Strategic Management. *Strategic Management Journal*, 13, pp. 363-380.

Makino, N. (1985). *Hanei to suibo (Decline and Prosperity)*, Tokyo: Kodansha.

Marsh, R.M. and Mannari, H. (1986). Entrepreneurship in Medium- and Large-Scale Japanese Firms. In Greenfield, S.M. and Strickon, A. (Eds.), *Entrepreneurship and Social Change*, Lanham, MD: University Press of America.

Maruyama, M. (1992). Interrelation Among Sciences, Politics, Asthetics, Business Management, and Economics. In Maruyama, M. (Ed.), *Context and Complexity. Cultivating Contextual Understanding*, New York: Springer, pp. 2-25.

Matsushita, K. (1989). *As I See It*, Tokyo: PHP Institute.

Mattsson, L.G. (1987). Management of Strategic Change in a Market As Networks Perspective. In Pettigrew, A.M. (Ed.), *The Management of Strategic Change*, Oxford, England: Oxford University Press, pp. 234-256.

Maturana, H.R. (1975). The Organization of the Living: A Theory of the Living Organization. *The International Journal of Man-Machine Studies*, 7, pp. 313-332.

Messner, D. (1997). *The Network Society: Economic Development and International Competitiveness As Problems of Social Governance*, London: Frank Cass.

Miles, R.E. and Snow, C.C. (1986). Organizations: New Concepts for New Firms. *California Management Review*, 28(2), pp. 62-73.

Mintzberg, H. (1989). *Mintzberg on Management: Inside Our Strange World of Organizations*, New York: The Free Press.

Miyashita, K. and Russel, D. W. (1994). *Keiretsu: Inside the Hidden Japanese Conglomerates*, New York: McGraw-Hill.

Monden, Y. (1991). *Shin Toyota Jisutemu (The New Toyota System)*, Tokyo: Kodansha.

Morgan, G. (1986). *Images of Organization*, Beverley Hills, CA: Sage.

Morikawa, H. (1992). *Zaibatsu. The Rise and Fall of Family Entreprises Groups in Japan*, Tokyo: University of Tokyo Press.

Morita, A. (1992). Partnering for Competitiveness: The Role of Japanese Business. *Harvard Business Review*, 70, May-June, pp. 76-83.

Müller, H.-E. (1997). Global Corporate Strategies and Local Interests? (On the Discussion in Europe). *Malaysian Management Journal*, 2(1), pp. 23-35.

Murakami, T. (1992). Kyosei and the Next Generation of Japanese-Style Management. *Nomura Research Institute Quarterly*, Winter, pp. 2-27.

Nadler, D.A. and Tushman, M.L. (1990). Beyond the Charismatic Leader: Entrepreneurship and Organizational Change. *California Management Review*, Winter, pp. 77-86.

Naisbitt, J. (1994). *Global Paradox*, New York: William Morrow.

Nakane, C. (1970). *Japanese Society*, Berkeley, CA: University of California Press.

Nakatani, I. (1990). *Effectiveness in Technological Innovation:* Keiretsu *versus Conglomerates*, Seattle: University of Washington Press, pp. 151-162.

Neumann, J. and Morgenstern, O. (1944). *Theory of Games and Economic Behavior*, Princeton, NJ: Princeton University Press.

Neves, T.M., Summe, G.L., and Uttal, B. (1990). Commercializing Technology: What the Best Companies Do. *Harvard Business Review*, 68, May-June, pp. 154-163.

Nielson, R.P. (1988). Cooperative Strategy. *Strategic Management Journal*, 9(3), pp. 475-492.

Nishiguchi, T. (1993). Supplier and Buyer Networks, Working Paper, MIT-IMVP.

Nodoushani, O. (1991). The End of the Entrepreneurial Age. *Human Systems Management*, 10, pp. 19-24.

Noguchi, Y. (1993). The Bubble Economy and Its Aftermath. In Kano, Y., Noguchi, Y., Saito, S., and Shimada, H. (Eds.), *The Japanese Economy in the 1990s: Problems and Prognoses*, Tokyo: Foreign Press Center, pp. 42-58.

Nohria, N. (1992). Is a Network Perspective a Useful Way of Studying Organizations? In Nohria, N. and Eccles, R.G. (Eds.), *Networks and Organizations: Structure, Form and Action*, Boston: Harvard University Press, pp. 1-22.

Nonaka, I. (1990). Managing Globalization As a Self-Renewing Process: Experiences of Japanese MNCs. In Barlett, C.A., Doz, Y., and Hedlund, G. (Eds.), *Managing the Global Firm*, London: Routledge, pp. 69-94.

Nonaka, I. and Johansson, J.K. (1985). Organizational Learning in Japanese Companies. In Lamb, R.B. (Ed.), *Advances in Strategic Management*, Greenwich, CT: JAI, pp. 23-46.

Nonaka, I. and Takeuchi, H. (1995). *The Knowledge-Creating Company*, Oxford, England: Oxford University Press.

Numagami, T., Ohta, T., and Nonaka, I. (1996). Self-Renewal of Corporate Organizations: Equilibrium, Self-Sustaining, and Self-Renewing Models. In Richter, F.-J. (Ed.), *The Dynamics of Japanese Organizations*, London: Routledge, pp. 9-31.

Odagiri, H. (1992). *Growth Through Competition, Competition Through Growth: Strategic Management and the Economy in Japan*, Oxford, England: Clarendon Press.

Ohmae, K. (1985). *Triad Power: The Coming Shape of Global Competition*, New York: The Free Press.

Ohmae, K. (1989). The Global Logic of Strategic Alliances. *Harvard Business Review*, March-April, pp. 143-154.

Okimoto, D.L. (1989). *Between MITI and the Market: Japanese Industrial Policy for High Technology*, Stanford, CA: Stanford University Press.

Okumura, H. (1981). *Mitsubishi-Nihon o ugokasu kigyoshudan—(Mitsubishi—the Corporate Group Which Moves Japan)*, Tokyo: Daiyamondo Gendai Sensho.

Orton, J.D. and Weick, K.E. (1990). Loosely Coupled Systems: A Reconceptualization. *Academy Management Review*, 15, pp. 203-223.

Ouchi, W. (1981). *Theory Z: How American Business Can Meet the Japanese Challenge*, Reading, MA: Addison-Wesley.

Park, S.-J., Gunther, I., and v.d. Osten, B. (1992). Japanese Management in West Germany: Results of the Second Enquete-Research. In Park, S.-J. (Ed.), *Managerial Efficiency in Competition and Cooperation*, Frankfurt, Germany/Boulder, CO: Campus/Westview, pp. 59-85.

Parkhe, A. (1992). Interfirm Diversity, Organizational Learning and Longevity, *Journal of International Business Strategies*, 3, pp. 579-601.

Pasternack, B.A. and Viscio, A.J. (1998). *The Centerless Corporation: A New Model for Transforming Your Organization for Growth and Prosperity*, New York: Simon & Schuster.

Pearce, D.W. and Warford, J.J. (1993). *World Without End: Economics, Environment, and Sustainable Development*, Oxford, England: Oxford University Press.

Penrose, E.P. (1959). *The Theory of the Growth of the Firm*, Oxford, England: Oxford University Press.

Peteraf, M. (1993). The Cornerstones of Competitive Advantage: A Resource-Based View. *Strategic Management Journal*, 14, pp. 179-191.

Pfeffer, J. and Salancik, G.R. (1978). *The External Control of Organizations*, New York: Harper & Row.

Phillips, D.C. (1987). *Philosophy, Science, and Social Inquiry*, Oxford, England: Pergamon Press.

Piaget, J. (1978). *Behavior and Evolution*, New York: Random House.

Pinchot, S. (1986). *Intrapreneuring*, New York: Harper & Row.

Poirier, C.C. and Reiter, S.E. (1996). *Supply Chain Optimization: Building the Strongest Total Business Network*, San Francisco: Berrett-Koehler Publications.

Popper, K. (1945). *The Open Society and Its Enemies, I: The Spell of Plato; II: The High Tide of Prophecy: Hegel, Marx, and the Aftermath*, London: Routledge & Kegan Paul.

Popper, K. (1963). *Conjectures and Refutations: The Growth of Scientific Knowledge*, London: Routledge & Kegan Paul.

Porter, M. (1980). *Competitive Strategy*, New York: The Free Press.

Porter, M. (1987). From Competitive Advantage to Corporate Strategy, *Harvard Business Review*, May/June 1987, pp. 43-59.

Powell, W.W. (1990). Neither Market nor Hierarchy: Network Forms of Organizations. In Cummings, L.L. and Staw, B.M. (Eds.), *Research in Organizational Behaviour*, Greenwich, CT: JAI, pp. 345-349.

Powell, W.W., Koput, K.W., and Smith-Doerr, L. (1996). Interorganizational Collaboration and the Locus of Innovation: Networks of Learning in Biotechnology. *Administrative Science Quarterly*, 41, pp. 116-145.

Procassini, A. (1995). *Competitors in Alliance. Industry Associations, Global Rivalries and Business-Government Relations*, Westport, CT: Quorum Books.

Pucik, V. (1988). Strategic Alliances, Organizational Learning, and Competitive Advantage: The HRM Agenda. *Human Resource Management*, 27(1), pp. 77-93.

Rabelloti, R. (1990). The Organization Variable in Developing Countries. In Ciciotti, E., Alderman, N., and Thwaites, A. (Eds.), *Technological Change in a Spatial Context: Theory, Empirical Evidence, and Policy*, New York: Springer, pp. 67-84.

Reading, B. (1992). *Japan. The Coming Collapse*. London: Weidenfeld and Nicolson.

Redding, S.G. (1994). Comparative Management Theory: Jungle, Zoo, or Fossil Bed? *Organization Studies*, 15(3), 323-359.

Reich, R.B. (1991). *The Work of Nations: Preparing Ourselves for 21st-Century Capitalism*, New York: Knopf.

Reich, R.B. and Mankin, E.D. (1986). Joint Ventures with Japan Give Away Our Future. *Harvard Business Review*, March-April, pp. 78-86.

Richter, F.-J. (1994). The Emergence of Corporate Alliance Networks. *Human Systems Management*, 13(1), pp. 19-26.

Richter, F.-J. (1997). Industrial Restructuring in Post-Deng China: Towards a Network Economy. Paper presented at the 14th Annual Conference of the Euro-Asian Management Studies Association, Metz, France.

Richter, F.-J. (Ed.) (1999). *Business Networks in Asia: Promises, Doubts, and Perspectives*, Westport, CT: Quorum.

Richter, F.-J. and Teramoto, Y. (1995). Interpreneurship: A New Management Concept from Japan. *Management International Review*, 35, Special Issue 2/1995, pp. 91-104.

Richter, F.-J. and Teramoto, Y. (1996). Population Ecology versus Network Dynamics: From Evolution to Co-evolution. In Richter, F.-J. (Ed.), *The Dynamics of Japanese Organizations*, London: Routledge, pp. 151-166.

Richter, F.-J. and Vettel, K. (1995). Successful Joint Ventures in Japan: Knowledge Transfer Through Organizational Learning. *Long-Range Planning*, 28(3), 37-45.

Richter, F.-J. and Wakuta, Y. (1993). Permeable Networks: A Future Option for the European and Japanese Car Industries. *European Management Journal*, 2, pp. 262-267.

Robinson, W.T. (1988). Sources of Market Pioneer Advantages: The Case of Industrial Goods Industries. *Journal of Management Review*, 15(1), pp. 87-94.

Roche, E.M. (1996). Strategic Alliances—An Entrepreneurial Approach to Globalization. *Journal of Global Information Management*, 4(1), pp. 34-35.

Sai, Y. (1995). *The Eight Core Values of the Japanese Businessman*, Binghamton, NY: International Business Press.

Salancik, G.R. (1995). WANTED: A Good Network Theory of Organization. *Administrative Science Quarterly*, 40 (June), pp. 345-349.

Santos Antonio, N. (1999). Markets and Networks: How they Operate in Asia. In Richter, F.-J. (Ed.), *Business Networks in Asia*, Westport, CT: Quorum (forthcoming).

Sakaiya, T. (1991). *The Knowledge-Value Revolution*, Tokyo: Kodansha.

Sako, M. (1992). *Prices, Quality, and Trust. Inter-Firm Relations in Britain & Japan*, Cambridge, England: Cambridge University Press.

Saxenian, A. (1990). Regional Networks and the Resurgence of the Silicon Valley. *California Management Review*, 33, pp. 89-112.

Schein, E.H. (1984). Coming to a New Awareness of Organizational Culture. *Sloan Management Review*, 47(4), pp. 3-16.

Scher, M.J. (1997). *Japanese Interfirm Networks and Their Main Banks*, New York: St. Martin's Press.

Schumpeter, J.A. (1934). *The Theory of Economic Development: An Inquiry into Profits, Capital, Credit, Interest, and the Business Cycle*, Cambridge, MA: Harvard Business Press.

Schumpeter, J.A. (1942). *Capitalism, Socialism, and Democracy*, New York: Harper & Row.

Senge, P. (1990). *The Fifth Dimension: The Art and Practice of the Learning Organization*, New York: Doubleday.

Senge, P. (1993). Internal Markets and Learning Organizations. In Halal, W.E., Geranmayeh, A., and Pourdehnad, J. (Eds.), *Internal Markets*, New York: John Wiley & Sons, pp. 87-105.

Serapio, M. (1995). Management Localization in Japanese Subsidiaries in the United States. In Shenkar, O. (Ed.), *Global Perspectives of Human Resource Management*, Englewood Cliffs, NJ: Prentice-Hall, pp. 211-225.

Shareff, R. (1991). Ecovision: A Entrepreneurship Theory for Innovative Organizations. *Organizational Dynamics*, 2, pp. 50-61.

Shimada, H. (1993). The Challenge to Japanese Management. In Kano, Y., Noguchi, Y., Saito, S., and Shimada, H. (Eds.), *The Japanese Economy in the 1990s: Problems and Prognoses*, Tokyo: Foreign Press Center Japan.

Shimizu, R. (1991). Vitalization of Internal Organization. *Keio Business Review*, 28, pp. 21-33.

Shimokawa, K. (1994). *The Japanese Automobile Industry—A Business History*, London: The Athlone Press.

Shin, D. and Kwon, K.-H. (1999). Demystifying Asian Business Networks: The Hierarchical Core of Korean Chaebols. In Richter, F.-J. (Ed.), *Business Networks in Asia*, Westport, CT: Quorum (forthcoming).

Simon, H. (1961). *Administrative Behavior*, Second Edition, New York: Macmillan.

Simon, H. (1983). *Reason in Human Affairs*, Stanford, CA: University of Stanford Press.

Smircich, L. (1983). Concepts of Culture and Organizational Analysis. *Administrative Science Quarterly*, 3, pp. 339-358.

Snow, C., Miles, R.E., and Coleman, H.J. (1992). Managing 21st Century Network Organizations. *Organizational Dynamics*, 21 (Winter), pp. 5-20.

Stam, A. (1992). New Patterns of Cooperation Among Enterprises in Japan. In Park, S.J. (Ed.), *Managerial Efficiency in Competition and Cooperation*, Frankfurt, Germany/Boulder, CO: Campus/Westview, pp. 127-139.

Sugimoto, Y. (1997). *An Introduction to Japanese Society*, Cambridge, England: Cambridge University Press.

Sydow, J. (1996). Flexible Specialization in Regional Networks: Experiences from the Financial Service Industry in Germany. In Staber, U.H., Schaefer, N.V., and Sharma, B. (Eds.), *Business Networks: Prospects for Regional Development*, Berlin/New York: de Gruyter, pp. 25-38.

Takamura, J. (1991). Kyoso Seisaka to Kigyo Group (Antitrust Policy and *Keiretsu*). In Koyama, H. (Ed.), *Nihon no Kigyo Group (Japanese Business Groups)*, Tokyo: Nihon Keizai Shinbunsha, pp. 25-37.

Takeda, Y. (1991). Cooperation of Government, Industry, and Academia in Research and Development Activities in Japan. *International Journal of Technology Management*, 6, pp. 450-458.

Tateisi, K. (1985). *The Eternal Venture Spirit. An Executive's Practical Philosophy*, Cambridge/Norwalk, England: Productivity Press.

Taylor, F.W. (1911). *Principles of Scientific Management*. New York: Harper & Row.

Teece, D.J. (1981). The Multinational Entreprise: Market Failure and Market Power Considerations. *Sloan Management Review*, 22, pp. 237-247.

Teramoto, Y. (1990). *Nettuwaku pawa (Network Power)*, Tokyo: NTT Press.

Teramoto, Y. (1993). *Gakushu suru soshiki (The Learning Organization)*, Tokyo: Shobunsha.

Teramoto, Y. and Iwasaki, N. (1991). Strategic Information Networks for Competitive Advantage: Conversion to Network Management. In Trevor, M. (Ed.), *International Business and the Management of Change*, Worcester, England: Avebury, pp. 211-232.

Teramoto, Y., Iwasaki, N., Takai, T., and Wakuta, Y. (1993). *Dai senryaku (Grand Strategy)*, Tokyo: JMAM.

Teramoto, Y, Richter, F.-J., and Iwasaki, N. (1993). Learning to Succeed: What European Firms Can Learn from Japanese Approaches to Strategic Alliances. *Creativity and Innovation Management*, 2(2), pp. 114-121.

Teramoto, Y., Richter, F.-J., Iwasaki, N., Takai, T., and Wakuta, Y. (1994). Global Strategy of Japanese Semiconductor Industry: Knowledge Creation through Strategic Alliances. In Campbell, N. and Burton, F. (Eds.), *Japanese Multinationals: Strategies and Management in the Global Kaisha*, London: Routledge, pp. 71-84.

Tezuka, H. (1997). Success As the Source of Failure? Competition and Cooperation in the Japanese Economy. *Sloan Management Review*, 38(2), pp. 83-93.

Thurow, L. (1996). *The Future of Capitalism: How Today's Economic Forces Shape Tomorrow's World*, New York: William Morrow & Company.

Tichy, N.M. (1980). A Social Network Perspective for Organizational Development. In Cummings, T.G. (Ed.), *Systems Theory for Organization Development*, Chichester: John Wiley & Sons, pp. 115-162.

Tirole, J. (1988). *The Theory of Industrial Organization*, Cambridge, England: Cambridge University Press.

Tokunaga, S., Altmann, N., and Demes, H. (Eds.) (1992). *New Impacts on Industrial Relations*, Munich, Germany: Iudicium.

Tselichtchev, I. (1994). Rethinking Inter-Firm Ties in Japan as a Factor of Competitiveness. In Schütte, H. (Ed.), *The Global Competitiveness of the Asian Firm*, London: Macmillan, pp. 49-70.

Tselichtchev, I. (1999). Japan-Style Intercompany Groups: Evolution in the Asian Economic Context. In Richter, F.-J. (Ed.), *Business Networks in Asia*, Westport, CT: Quorum (forthcoming).

Ueda, Y. (1986). Intercorporate Networks in Japan. *Shoken Keizai*, 157, pp. 236-254.

Ueda, Y. (1991). Types and Characteristics of Interlocking Directorates in Japan. In Hamilton, G. (Ed.), *Business Networks and Economic Development in East and*

Southeast Asia, Hong Kong: Centre of Asian Studies, University of Hong Kong, pp. 230-243.

Uzzi, B. (1997). Social Structure and Competition in Interfirm Networks: The Paradox of Embeddedness. *Administrative Science Quarterly*, 42, pp. 35-67.

Van de Ven, A.H., Walker, G., and Liston, J. (1979). Coordination Patterns Within an Interorganizational Network. *Human Relations*, 32 (1), pp. 19-36.

Van de Ven, A.H. and Walker, G. (1984). The Dynamics of Interorganizational Coordination. *Administrative Science Quarterly*, 29, pp. 598-621.

Van Wolferen, K. (1989). *The Enigma of Japanese Power: The First Full Scale Examination of the Inner Workings of Japan's Political/Industrial System*, New York: Knopf.

Vogel, E.F. (1979). *Japan As Number One: Lessons for America*, Cambridge, MA: Harvard University Press.

Von Bertalanffy, L. (1962). *Modern Theories of Development*, New York: Harper Torchbooks.

Walsh, J.P. and Ungson, G.R. (1991). Organizational Memory, *Academy of Management Review*, 1, pp. 157-191.

Weber, M. (1993). *Basic Concepts in Sociology*, New York: Citadel Press.

Weick, K.E. (1969). *The Social Psychology of Organizing*, Reading, MA: Addison-Wesley.

Weick, K.E. (1976). Educational Organizations As Loosely Coupled Systems. *Administration Science Quarterly*, 21, pp. 1-19.

Weick, K.E. (1987). Organizational Culture As a Source of High Reliability. *California Management Review*, 29, 112-127.

Weidenbaum, M. and Hughes, S. (1996). *The Bamboo Network: How Expatriate Chinese Entrepreneurs Are Creating a New Economic Superpower in Asia,* New York: The Free Press.

Williamson, O.E. (1975). *Markets and Hierarchies: Analysis and Antitrust Implications*, New York: The Free Press.

Williamson, O.E. (1985). *The Economic Institutions of Capitalism*, New York: The Free Press.

Womack, J., Jones, D., and Ross, D. (1990). *The Machine That Changed the World*, New York: Rawson Associates.

Wood, C. (1992). *The Bubble Economy: The Japanese Economic Collapse*, London: Sidwick & Jackson.

Yamamura, K. (1971). The Origins of Entrepreneurship in Meiji Japan. In Kilby, P. (Ed.), *Entrepreneurship and Economic Development*, New York: The Free Press, pp. 267-286.

Yasumono, K. (1993). Engineers As Functional Alternative to Entrepreneurs in Japan's Industrialization. In Brown, J. (Ed.), *Entrepreneurship, Networks and Modern Business*, Manchester, England: Manchester University Press, pp. 76-84.

Yip, G.S. (1992). *Total Global Strategy: Managing for Worldwide Competitive Advantage*, Englewood Cliffs, NJ: Prentice-Hall.

Yip, G.S. (1998). *Asian Advantage. Key Strategies for Winning in the Asia-Pacific Region*, New York: Perseus Books.

Yoshihara, H. (1989). The Bright and the Dark Sides of Japanese Management Overseas. In Shibagaki, K., Trevor, M., and Abo, T. (Eds.), *Japanese and European Management*, Tokyo: Tokyo University Press, pp. 18-30.

Yoshihara, K. (1988). *The Rise of Ersatz Capitalism in South-East Asia*, Singapore: Oxford University Press.

Yoshinari, M. (1992). The Big Six Horizontal *Keiretsu*. *Japan Quarterly*, 39, pp. 186-199.

Yoshino, M.Y. and Rangan, U.S. (1995). *Strategic Alliances: An Entrepreneurial Approach to Globalization*, Boston: Harvard Business Press.

Young, A.K. (1979). *The Sogo Shosha. Japan's Multinational Trading Companies*, Boulder, CO: Westview Press.

Zahra, S., Garvis, D., and George, G. (1999). Networks and Entrepreneurship: The Role of Social Capital and Membership Commitment. In Richter, F.-J. (Ed.), *Business Networks in Asia*, Westport, CT: Quorum, (forthcoming).

Zeleny, M. (1990) Amoeba: The New Generation of Self-Managing Human Systems. *Human Systems Management*, 9(2), pp. 57-69.

Zeleny, M. (1996). Comparitive Management Systems: Trade-Offs-Free Concept. In Richter, F.-J. (Ed.), *The Dynamics of Japanese Organizations*, London: Routledge, pp. 167-177.

Zeleny, M., Cornet, R., and Stoner, J.A.F. (1990). Moving from the Age of Specialization to the Era of Integration. *Human Systems Management*, 9, pp. 153-171.

Index

Page numbers followed by the letter "f" indicate figures.

Order Your Own Copy of
This Important Book for Your Personal Library!

STRATEGIC NETWORKS
The Art of Japanese Interfirm Cooperation

_____in hardbound at $49.95 (ISBN: 0-7890-0725-8)

COST OF BOOKS_____	☐ **BILL ME LATER:** ($5 service charge will be added) (Bill-me option is good on US/Canada/Mexico orders only; not good to jobbers, wholesalers, or subscription agencies.)
OUTSIDE USA/CANADA/ MEXICO: ADD 20%_____	
POSTAGE & HANDLING_____ (US: $3.00 for first book & $1.25 for each additional book) Outside US: $4.75 for first book & $1.75 for each additional book)	☐ Check here if billing address is different from shipping address and attach purchase order and billing address information. Signature_____
SUBTOTAL_____	☐ **PAYMENT ENCLOSED: $**_____
IN CANADA: ADD 7% GST_____	☐ **PLEASE CHARGE TO MY CREDIT CARD.**
STATE TAX_____ (NY, OH & MN residents, please add appropriate local sales tax)	☐ Visa ☐ MasterCard ☐ AmEx ☐ Discover ☐ Diner's Club
FINAL TOTAL_____ (If paying in Canadian funds, convert using the current exchange rate. UNESCO coupons welcome.)	Account #_____ Exp. Date_____ Signature_____

Prices in US dollars and subject to change without notice.

NAME _____

INSTITUTION _____

ADDRESS _____

CITY _____

STATE/ZIP _____

COUNTRY _____ COUNTY (NY residents only) _____

TEL _____ FAX _____

E-MAIL_____

May we use your e-mail address for confirmations and other types of information? ☐ Yes ☐ No

Order From Your Local Bookstore or Directly From
The Haworth Press, Inc.
10 Alice Street, Binghamton, New York 13904-1580 • USA
TELEPHONE: 1-800-HAWORTH (1-800-429-6784) / Outside US/Canada: (607) 722-5857
FAX: 1-800-895-0582 / Outside US/Canada: (607) 772-6362
E-mail: getinfo@haworthpressinc.com
PLEASE PHOTOCOPY THIS FORM FOR YOUR PERSONAL USE.

BOF96